A LIGHT IN THE TUNNEL

To My Mother Ayşegül Betíl
And To My Father Tímur Selçuk
With Gratitude...

A LIGHT IN THE TUNNEL

FINDING YOUR WAY THROUGH ANXIETY AND DEPRESSION

HAZAL SELÇUK, LMFT

LEAP FROG PRESS

A LIGHT IN THE TUNNEL

Finding Your Way Through Anxiety and Depression

Editors:
John Grey, PhD
Susan Campbell, PhD

Publisher:
Leap Frog Press
501 Swain Avenue
Sebastopol, CA 95472

Author:
hazalselcuk.com

TABLE OF CONTENTS

Exercises

 ***The flower marks the start of an exercise...***

Some exercises include an online audio to guide you. Access all the online audios at this location:

hazalselcuk.com/tunnel-exercises

INTRODUCTION

Depression or anxiety can feel like getting stuck in a deep, dark tunnel. Overwhelmed by darkness, we yearn to see the light at the *end* of the tunnel. Many of us can remain stuck for so long we may even worry that we'll never see it.

I propose a different take on this familiar tunnel metaphor. Let's bring light *into* the tunnel. Instead of waiting to someday find a light out in the future, let's learn to bring light into the overwhelming symptoms of anxiety or depression—and to use it to see how to move forward.

In today's world, we encounter many types of stressors. Our personal challenges can combine with economic, societal, and planetary issues. Pandemic surges, climate crises, social injustice, or inability to find satisfying work opportunities all can impact our physical, emotional and mental resources.

Dealing with such overwhelming things takes an energetic toll. Our tolerance for stress is reduced. We may find ourselves easily getting anxious, frustrated or exhausted.

We may sense a loss of control, feeling victimized or powerless. In an attempt to find relief, we may engage in some self-destructive behaviors that deepen our sense of helplessness.

Overwhelmed, we may feel like we will never regain any kind of inner peace, balance or control.

Part of the solution is to get some clarity—the kind of clarity that leads us to increased understanding and containment. The situation thereby can become more manageable. Even in the face of extreme pressures coming from the external environment, how we relate to our internal experience will affect its impact on us.

The Clinical Perspective

If you have been suffering from fatigue or low energy, a depressed mood, loss of motivation, loss of interest or enjoyment, a change in sleep or appetite, poor concentration, feelings of worthlessness, or suicidal thoughts, then you are familiar with some of the heavy symptoms of depression.

Symptoms of anxiety that impair quality of living may include sleep disturbances, uncontrolled worrying, poor concentration, irritability, becoming easily fatigued, or muscle tension.

Such symptoms might also be caused in part by a physical illness or side effects of medications. Please consult a doctor before self-diagnosing. Everything in the body is connected. Any of a number of medical conditions can amplify or even cause the symptoms described above.

I will begin this book by presenting an alternate clinical view of depression and anxiety. I will reframe these conditions as life energy that becomes jumbled in the face of overwhelm.

I use the term "life energy" to refer to the energetic activity of our nervous system, including the moment-to-moment arousal or activation level and how that impacts our bodily, our mental and our emotional functioning.

This life energy can spin out in two possible directions. If it goes to depression, the energy gets shut down and frozen. If anxiety, the energy becomes amped up and scattered.

As two sides of a coin, depression and anxiety can even coexist within us. We may switch from one state to the other as our nervous system tries to manage overwhelm.

This book will help you recognize and track the movement of your life energy within, and how doing this can illuminate a way forward. I will show you how to learn from depression or anxiety and increase your capacity to deal with overwhelm.

The Artistic Perspective

A common tendency is to relate to art as a leisure time thing to take in for entertainment. In that view, we can feel comfortable in the audience that takes in artistic expression—be it in theater, movies, music, dance, writing, or the visual arts.

But taking the position of creating art would be quite another matter. Being asked to *produce* it likely would evoke discomfort. We believe that to be solely the province of trained, professional artists.

So first and foremost, I want to assure you that nothing in this book is about trying to be an "artist" or to produce "art".

It is about you gaining access to and experiencing the benefits of engaging in the *process* of creativity—not the *product*. The main benefit being to discover ways to transform your own inner states.

So this is solely for you—not for anybody else. There is no audience. Nothing you have to perform. No art product to produce.

It's entirely about opening up new doors to what you can experience within yourself.

The *process* of creativity in the arts is what I will help you explore. It offers an excellent toolkit to look inside and touch deeper emotional dynamics, and to begin transforming and healing them.

A Cry of the Soul

When I look at depression or anxiety through an artistic lens, I view these conditions as a cry of the soul. But unlike actual crying—where energy can get released and transformed—we become stuck.

In that the arts are largely about processing and transforming thoughts and feelings through the creative endeavor, an artistic perspective can offer new ways of seeing and being with these conditions.

Of course, the definition of "soul" is subjective, nonlinear, and complex. My personal interpretation of soul is my center, the essence which has been with me since I have known myself. This was me when I was three years old and now feels the same, even though I have aged and evolved.

That pure essence is what connects me to an intelligence larger than myself. When I close my eyes and sense into myself, I get in touch with something larger than my personality, my profession, or the many other things that commonly form my sense of identity.

This center within me feels timeless.

I propose that depression and anxiety are symptoms that reflect a cry from this inner essence. This is very much like a signal cry wanting to deliver a message that has a greater meaning about our life purpose and about who we are.

I will show you a variety of ways to better hear and work with this cry of depression or anxiety using nonlinear artistic means that involve music, theater, movement and drawing.

I have found that as we become more willing to start listening for this inner message, we can begin to transform painful emotional experiences.

My Personal Journey

Why is it that I combine these two perspectives, the clinical and the artistic, to better understand how to work with depression and anxiety? In many ways, it is a reflection of my own journey.

Growing up in Istanbul, I came from a family of three generations of performance artists. My mother was a dancer. Both my father and grandfather were composers and singers. My grandmother was an actress. Having lived with so many artists, naturally, I became one myself.

I know the experience of magic on stage and the stress behind stage. I know the difficulties of making a living as an artist, the lack of grants, the stress of marketing and management, the loneliness that can come out of only wanting to do work I believe in, but having to deal with royalty issues or political issues, just to name a few common sources of stress.

I thought these were generational issues specific to Turkey. But over time, having lived in Austria, France, Canada and the United States, and having worked with artists from many different parts of the world, I can now say that most of these issues are in fact universal.

Of course, I am also very familiar with that deep physical, emotional, and spiritual connection to self and others that can be experienced in the process of making art and when engaging in performance.

I experienced the therapeutic power of the arts on many levels—as a multimodal performance artist who sang, danced, acted, and created original works. I felt this healing power through vocal work as well as in movement work. I also experienced it through acting and in the process of creating pieces.

When I was on stage, I felt grounded, calm and connected. I felt very present. I could trust myself. My heart was open to connection. When I was off stage, I wanted to work in the studio and prepare for that connectedness that I experienced on stage.

At some point, I noticed that when I wasn't on stage or in the studio, then I also was not as present or connected to myself or others.

It seemed like I only allowed myself to be *me* in the studio or on stage. And I was living my daily life as if it was a preparation for being on stage, as if the "the real thing" was only available on stage.

I noticed myself wishing that my daily life involved more of the kind of connectedness I felt on stage and in the studio.

I wanted more presence within myself and with others, more emotional openness, trust, spontaneity, creativity, curiosity, and more love for being alive to become a part of my ordinary life.

I have known many artists who, although capable of creating great beauty in their art, were still very emotionally unaware or self-destructive in their daily lives. I have also seen those on a true path of evolution using their art daily as a healing tool.

I have personally lost loved ones to extreme depression. Some were artists and some not. But the common thread was how much pain they were in and how difficult it was for them to ask for or to receive support.

This book comes out of the pain and helplessness I felt when I witnessed loved ones in distress. I think partly what led me on the path of bringing the arts and therapy together was that pain.

This book comes from a desire to help the people I love who have already passed away. I hope now that it can bring some relief to all those who want it.

Integrating the Arts and Therapy

Many years ago, I suffered from depression. It was not clinical depression, but it was still painful. Hearing well-intentioned loved ones encourage me to "just get up and do something" didn't help.

Yet, when I discovered a certain way of being within myself, the symptoms would lessen.

My medicine became the arts. I wrote poetry. I made theater pieces. I drew. I sang. I engaged in movement improvisation and somatic work.

As a result, for the past fifteen years I have not experienced depression. When I feel "down" I now can stop and listen.

It was the process of artmaking to deal with my own pain which initially led me study psychology and to become a therapist.

As I worked with artists, students, and later with patients and clients from different parts of the world, I witnessed over and over again that the human heart always has the same longing: *connection.*

Connection can be a loaded word.

Whether this refers to connecting to a purpose, a living being, or to oneself, immense pain stems from the lack of it.

Years ago I remember a student of mine telling me that she longed for someone who could bring her out of a dark tunnel she felt inside of herself, a place where she was hiding.

She said she wanted to be able to fully be herself. When I asked what that meant to her, she said that she wanted to be able to laugh, cry or be angry when she needed to do so. She said that she wanted to open her arms wide to the sky, and not to be afraid.

She asked me, "Could you help me open my arms to the sky without fear?" So, we started working on that theme—using the arts—and over time it turned into a solo piece.

How can the arts have this power to heal?

In this book, I'll guide you to engage in creative conversations within yourself. This will help you to embody more inner listening that also opens space for self-expression in many forms.

When we get to the heart of the book, I will also include short exercises so you can experience these concepts from the inside out. Some of the exercises also offer online audio recordings that will guide you as you listen to them.

In the last part of the book I will briefly discuss a 21-day program designed to more specifically work with the symptoms of depression and anxiety. That program is available online as a series of audios that give you step-by-step guidance.

My personal viewpoint is that as depression and anxiety are actually messages from the soul, they are not things to fear or to cause us to feel shame.

These symptoms are asking for a listener.

Who is that listener?

You.

You might feel as if you have gotten lost in an endless tunnel. This book is designed to give you a *light* to help see the path and how to move forward, to hear what the symptoms of anxiety or depression are actually trying to tell you.

Are you willing to lend an ear to yourself?

I am often asked if being an artist is required for this approach to work. Absolutely not.

You do not need to be an artist to benefit. But by engaging in the creative process, you will be able to take advantage of the way many artists transform their pain into beauty.

Certainly, it is clear that the art industry is in no way oriented towards providing psychotherapy. Yet art itself can be therapeutic because it fosters freedom to engage in nonlinear, nonjudgmental forms of self-exploration and self-expression.

Art makes an open space for intuitive ways of self-knowing.

By contrast, traditional psychotherapy typically offers analytic or medical approaches to address human suffering. Those can provide useful resources to better view and understand symptoms.

Taken together, however, the arts and psychology—integrating nonlinear and linear, intuitive and analytic approaches—offer a powerful combination for healing.

The intuitively sensing, emotion-based expressive nature of the arts, combined with the scientific, analytical knowledge of psychology, taken together encompass more complexity of the human heart, mind, body and soul.

In a nutshell, that is what this book is about.

As I have experienced the power of both the arts and therapy, this book combines clinical and artistic approaches for working with anxiety or depression. My intention is to offer new ways to be with yourself that foster both self-expression and self-healing.

Chapter 1

The Complexity of Depression and Anxiety

"There is no meaning to life. But I hear a slight whisper that makes me wonder that, maybe, I am wrong."
— SAID BY A CLIENT IN OUR FIRST SESSION

What do most of us do when we are depressed or anxious? We want to get rid of it. Naturally. Some of us think about medication. Others consider going to a therapist. Either way, the intention is for it to be *gone.*

We want to return to *normal.*

Few of us question what in our so-called "normal" may have led to depression or anxiety in the first place. Seldom do we get curious about what drives depression or anxiety in us.

In this chapter we will look at depression and anxiety in terms of differing energy levels in our nervous system. Tracking the movement of life energy is a very useful way of identifying where your system is at.

Let's start with depression…

Here are some of its many voices:

"I sunk so deep in the ocean it's hard to breathe."
"I want to live underground. Not bother anyone."
"There is so much wrong with me."
"I am just too lazy."
"It feels like my leg fell asleep, only it's my soul."

Depression is experienced as an internal state.

It is a difficult place to be when it is the only one available. It impairs us from taking action, whether that's a step towards what we want, or moving away from what we don't want.

When we are depressed we have little access to motivation or to a sense of agency. We have the idea that the basic human drive "to want" something is blocked. We entertain negative thoughts that reach a single conclusion:

"I can't..."

When we are experiencing symptoms of depression it feels nearly impossible to get in touch with thoughts that fuel any sense of *"I can!"*

When depressed, it seems like there is a negative judge sitting on our shoulder. The judge would point out all that is impossible, finding us guilty of deficiency.

If you had a friend talking like this judge, you would most likely want to end that conversation. However, when operating subliminally inside your mind, this judge can have a lot of power. It tells you things like:

"You don't deserve to..."
"You can never..."
"What is wrong with you!"
"You have wasted your life..."
"It is not safe to trust anyone..."

It is like dark clouds overtaking the sky and the sun seems to disappear. In this darkness, it feels like we are stuck, trapped, or sunken down so deep that we don't have the energy to care.

At this stage, many people take on that judge's voice and continue to blame themselves. Or they blame their environment including the people in it in a way that continues to energize the inner message: *"I am powerless."*

This adds further stress to the already existing state of overwhelm. And depression is an automatic reaction to overwhelm that is trying to protect us from feeling deeper layers of emotional pain.

The nervous system is so overloaded by distress and unable to express it that a "shut down" mode takes over in order to preserve our life energy.

But this has a cost. Believing our thoughts and taking our current internal state as the only reality possible, we lose access to our actual ability to think or feel in a way that fosters relief and transformation. Unconsciously we continue digging ourselves further into the tunnel.

The Experience of Anxiety

Like depression, the symptoms of anxiety are overwhelming. Here are some of its many expressions:

"I can never find time to rest, I'm so worried."
"I am afraid people will hate me if they know me."
"I am sure something will go wrong."
"No one has my back, I am all alone."
"I am afraid I will make the wrong decision."
"Inside me is like a screeching electric guitar...
And I can't turn it off."

Ongoing anxiety is the nervous system's inability to return to a state of calm. It is like the lights stay on full time, overamped and flashing. There is no ability to rest or relax. The radar is always on, the threat alarm continually ringing. Imagine a guard without any sleep or rest, who is always on duty.

Normally fear is a healthy and useful signal that something might be dangerous. It serves as a warning sign so one can orient and check if there is a threat. And then, if there is a threat, we assess how serious the threat is.

That fear signal motivates us to move forward to fight, or go into flight to escape the threat. Once we identify that there is no longer a threat, then our nervous system is meant to shift back into a state of calm.

Our nature is built for action and rest, excitement and relaxation. We are meant to return to a state of calm after having dealt with the distress.

However, sometimes the source of threat cannot be clearly identified. Sometimes the action of fighting or fleeing is not possible. Then the energy will stay amped up in our nervous system.

There will be no resolution.

Life energy cannot find a direction, movement, or release. The energy gets caught in a feedback loop that keeps us cycling around in unresolved fear and hypervigilance.

This corresponds to anxiety.

The Energy of Safety vs Danger

Depression and anxiety can be seen as different ways our nervous system reacts to perceived danger or to getting overwhelmed. In the chart below, the horizontal axis is the passing of time and the vertical axis is the level of energy in our nervous system.

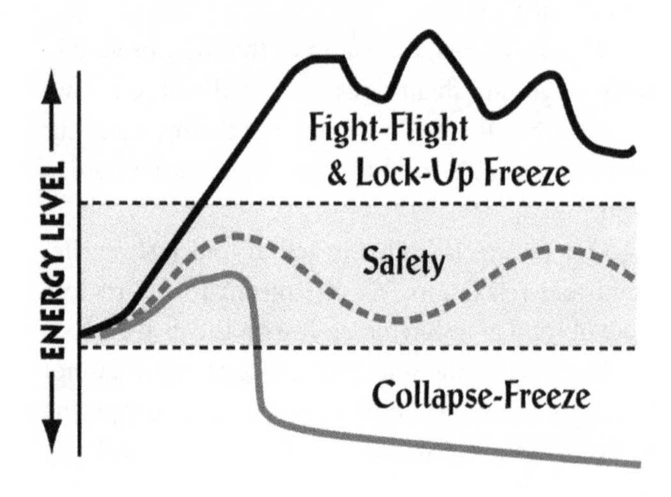

In the safety zone of the chart, we experience the ongoing ups and downs of daily life with increased energy and recovery, action and resting. This optimal zone of energetic functioning gives us access to our full set of mental and emotional resources.

But if we sense danger or adverse circumstances, our system will get amped up into a hyperaroused state of fight or flight. If we are unable to take action or find resolution, we can then get locked up or frozen in high arousal. This corresponds to anxiety.

If the sense of danger is extremely overwhelming, and there is no escape, we can shut down into a hypoaroused state of collapsed freeze or numbing. That corresponds to depression.

Much of the time, symptoms of anxiety and depression reflect unconscious management strategies to avoid overwhelm or emotional pain. In an attempt to find relief, we unconsciously keep ourselves in states of panic or shutdown—anxiety or depression. We may even swing back and forth between these states like a pendulum.

The Impact of Trauma

Closely related to feeling unsafe, a common cause of depression and anxiety is trauma. Trauma is the residual impact of a shocking, overwhelming event (or set of events) on the nervous system.

We can differentiate two basic types of trauma—*shock trauma* and *developmental trauma.*

Shock trauma arises from an event that occurs too quickly or is energetically too much for our nervous system to respond to, manage or integrate. This overwhelms our capacity to act and that then leaves us stuck with feelings of fear, danger, threat, helplessness, and a loss of control.

As examples, getting attacked by a wild animal or being involved in a car accident can result in a state of utter shock and loss of control. If the event poses (or seems to pose) a direct threat to our life, and we can't fight or flee, our nervous system will plummet into freeze.

Shock trauma can also result from threatening interactions with other people. War, rape, physical assault, robbery, or other such events can easily trigger overwhelm in the nervous system.

A difference between shock trauma and developmental trauma is that in the former, I don't have an attachment to the threatening figure. Thus, pure shock trauma mostly impacts my physiology but not my sense of self.

If a bear attacks me, I have no emotional bonding or investment with the bear. If I am hit by a car, I have no emotional attachment to the driver. In these kinds of cases, if I experience helplessness and can't fight or flee, my nervous system automatically will go into a freeze—but my *sense of self* will not be significantly impacted.

However, if I experience sexual assault, both my physiology and my sense of self might be impacted. Certainly, if I experience a traumatic event that involves someone to whom I am emotionally attached, the impact will be quite severe.

If that occurs when I am very young, it will likely result in what we call a developmental trauma.

Developmental trauma is caused by attachment injuries that took place in childhood. Examples are neglect and ongoing physical or emotional abuse. In developmental trauma the survival threat is linked to an attachment figure the child loves and depends on.

The one who is supposed to make the child feel safe is posing a threat to his sense of safety. The caregiver turns into a scare-giver. Therefore, developmental trauma disrupts not only nervous system homeostasis, but also the child's sense of self.

In developmental trauma, a child has to choose between the self and the attachment relationship. He cannot have both. He cannot be himself and keep the attachment relationship.

In order to preserve the attachment relationship, the child abandons his own needs which means that he can no longer genuinely move towards what he wants or move away from what he doesn't want.

Depending on the developmental level of the child, he may no longer feel safe to feel his emotions, to express his needs, to set boundaries, to explore or claim autonomy, or to depend on others.

He may conclude that he is not enough and that he is not inherently valuable or loveable unless he performs or is perfect.

For a child, attachment equates to survival.

Therefore, ongoing misattunements, abuse, or neglect are life-threatening. Both the physiology and psychology of the child get severely impacted. Since a child cannot flee or fight the holding environment, she has to do her best to adapt.

A neglected baby's nervous system will initially register neglect as shock which, through repetition, will turn into developmental trauma.

If, as an adult, I get physically attacked by my partner—as opposed to a stranger—this can impact both my physiology *and* my sense of self, creating a more complex trauma, similar in kind to developmental trauma.

And a shock trauma could also trigger an earlier developmental trauma, which can make it far more complex to process.

Animal Survival Responses

Let's review the states of fight, flight, and freeze through the lens of animal survival responses.

In the face of a traumatic event, any mammal will attempt to defend itself through a series of survival responses. These are animal defenses and they are an integral part of our survival instincts.

Possible survival responses are: *startle, orienting, signal cry, fight, flight,* and *freeze.*

If you have ever witnessed animals in dangerous situations, you probably saw them using one or more of these defenses in order to survive.

The *startle* response shows sensing of danger.

The *orienting* response exhibits the attempt to identify where and what that threat is.

The *signal cry* is a call for help.

The *fight* response shows aggressive behaviors deemed necessary or possible to overcome a threat, or when flight is unavailable or unsuccessful.

The *flight* response exhibits escape behaviors. It can be used if fighting seems unlikely to succeed or when direct confrontation is not possible.

Freeze is an unconscious animal defense which results in immobility. This happens automatically whenever the level of activation reaches a certain threshold in the nervous system.

The freeze response has a sense of being stuck, paralyzed, or unable to move or breathe. Here the nervous system falls into a state of *collapse* which can evoke low arousal, numbness, depression, absence, blankness, fainting, giving up, or sinking.

There is another animal defense response that results in a condition of frozen immobility. We refer to this state as *lock-up* freeze. It carries high energy and tension, where an animal feels a very strong impulse to move, but instead gets locked up.

Lock-up could be seen as getting frozen between fight and flight. This type of immobility can occur if danger is still at a distance and staying motionless may prevent detection. An example is a deer in the headlights.

In nature, both types of freeze could potentially offer life-saving benefits in face of threat or danger. Not moving can keep one from being detected by a predator. It can also cause a predator to lose interest. For instance, consider an immobilized mouse being held in a cat's mouth. It is on the very threshold of life and death.

However, the cat could put the mouse down. If the mouse remains motionless for long enough, the cat might lose interest and walk away. That way the mouse's life will be saved.

If it was in the hyperaroused state of immobility, it will detect the cat leaving and quickly flee. But if it fell into the numb freeze state of collapse, it might then gradually awaken and escape.

In a collapsed state of freeze, the heart rate slows down, blood pressure drops, muscles soften into a vegetative state, the mind and body get numb, and memory storage is impaired. These are physiological responses that mimic death, potentially fooling the cat into dropping the mouse and even leaving.

But the state of collapse freeze offers another big benefit to the mouse. It corresponds to an internal state of anesthesia which will numb the mouse from experiencing bodily pain.

If the predator is fooled—like when the cat is no longer interested in the mouse and walks away—the mouse will eventually come out of freeze, connect with its life energy and go into flight, running away and hiding.

Note that the life energy has been present all along. It has just been inaccessible due to the collapse response of the nervous system to save the mouse's life in the face of extreme danger.

From this viewpoint, anxiety is seen as getting locked up in a continuous state of hyperarousal and depression can be seen as a persistent hypoaroused collapse response.

The nervous system and psyche are trying their best to manage the physiological and emotional overwhelm of a series of events or interpersonal injuries by going into hyper or hypoarousal.

So we can see that anxiety and depression initially come out of protective animal survival responses in the face of apparent danger, overwhelming life circumstances or threat.

However, when these animal defense response states last too long, it will result in a number of adverse symptoms. What was once a survival response will become a block to our well-being. Ongoing freeze states can impair memory, create a sense of hopelessness, and promote continued passive immobility under which the life energy will remain buried.

Loss of Hope

In states of anxiety or depression many people report that there is no sense of hope. What is hope?

Our minds are designed to predict. We make projections into the future based on our experiences in the past. We typically project more of what we have experienced. Or we may long for what we have not experienced.

Hope is an internal and external resource that enhances life. It can entail wanting, longing, or dreaming. Hope gives us an ability to project positivity into the future. We can become enchanted by future possibilities. Hope is energizing.

Hope can be a thought, a sense, a belief in change, an energizing longing. It can include a sense of relief or trust. It can evoke feelings of being supported, of energetic flow, and of positive possibilities.

When there is lack of hope, we cannot easily access our natural resilience or resourcefulness. Our resources seem to get locked up, frozen, and out of reach.

Therefore depression often results in an overwhelming sense of internal loneliness and helplessness. Anxiety shows up as helplessness and a desperate need to identify threat and to control the environment.

Restoring Resiliency

To restore our resiliency we need to reconnect to our internal and external resources. One way we establish internal resources as children is through imitating external role models, such as caregivers.

Other models can include teachers and peers. Through interactions and imitation, we develop representations of our caregivers, teachers, and best friends inside ourselves.

Our capacity to calm ourselves in distress is initially developed in early childhood through the holding we experienced with adults, especially our primary caregivers. We internally hold ourselves now the way we were held emotionally by them.

But if, as children, we were not held effectively when we were in distress, then in times of distress as adults, we may not know how to be within ourselves. We won't know how to contain or express our feelings, how to extend support to our self, or how to reach out for help from others.

In the face of unresolved emotional overwhelm, our nervous system may go into a state of startle, locked up in high-arousal immobility, or into a state of freeze, numbness, collapse, and shut down. Survival responses are unconscious and automatic. We don't choose them consciously.

But when we are aware of how our physiology operates under conditions of high distress, we can begin to discover how to work with ourselves. We can help our system by expanding our capacity to be with ourselves and containing deeper feelings that are present within us.

Doing this, we can create an internal resiliency so that the symptoms of depression or anxiety no longer automatically take over in an attempt to establish a sense of safety.

For some of us connecting to ourselves deeply does not feel safe. While part of us longs for a more connected way of being, another part of us might fear it. Navigating this dynamic gently and consciously can be a rich, transformative process.

In the next chapter I will talk about one of the most important aspects of unconscious navigation that is how we make meaning of overwhelming events.

CHAPTER 2

STORYMAKING AND MEANING-MAKING

"To the Wise, pain and grace are the same thing."
— SUFI SAYING

It is human to seek the meaning of things. The arts emerged out of a need to give meaning to our lives. For instance, in film and theater, we observe the characters' drama and how they respond to it.

From the audience we project parts of ourselves onstage. As we observe, feel, wonder, question, or interpret we are engaging in inquiry, giving meaning to what we see and how we respond to it.

Doing this is an act of embracing the complexity of our internal and external worlds. It is an antidote to rigidity. This kind of inquiry is fueled by our natural curiosity and meaning-making, and it fosters our sense of agency and fulfillment.

The need for meaning-making can take a very different turn in the face of overwhelming life events, especially in childhood. Our memory system, along with our ability to speak, begins to develop when we are about eighteen months old. Before then, our experience is purely somatic and nonverbal.

Memory and the child's ability to make meaning keeps developing into adulthood. A child's capacity to verbalize their feelings or thoughts will evolve through interactions with caregivers, teachers, and peers. It begins with simple meaning-making and evolves into an ability to hold increasing degrees of complexity.

The child starts with differentiating "good vs bad." Reading a fairy tale, she will associate Snow White with good, and feels sad when Snow White takes a bite of the poisonous apple. She enjoys the dwarves. She sees the witch as evil.

An adult reading the story might have a broader perspective and find a variety of meanings in the story. They might interpret the apple as the hardships in life we all have to bite into and digest. These help us to grow and evolve.

The time Snow White spends in sleep might be interpreted as a period of introspection, a time where she gets in touch with deeper parts of herself. Or it could be interpreted as disconnection from the self, falling into a sleep state to avoid confronting challenges.

The dwarves, the prince and the witch could be seen as representing parts inside of Snow White, all having messages to deliver to help her become more whole.

When the prince arrives and kisses her, and she wakes up, the adult might interpret that she has finally accessed a part of herself that helps her gain inner resilience and wake up to reality in a new way with more agency.

Making Meaning of Trauma

In the face of overwhelming circumstances, the meaning we attribute to an event will depend on our ability to hold complexity in our minds, hearts and bodies. That is no small task.

The analytic brain formulates linear stories in order to make meaning of feelings, pictures, people, events and sensations. These stories generate beliefs.

In a child's brain, when she feels bad inside, such as feeling pain in her heart or a knot in her stomach, her simple neural wiring will probably not be able to generate a story complex enough to include an accurate assessment of her environment.

If she is then unable to get support from an adult brain to make sense of what her "feeling bad" actually means, the child's brain will automatically create simplistic negative stories.

These stories will involve the child's sense of self and result in negative beliefs about herself. The child will not be able to differentiate *feeling* bad from *being* bad. Whenever she feels bad she will also believe that she *is* bad.

This is at the root of developmental trauma. The child's brain might generate beliefs like:

"I am no good."
"I am just trash."
"I will always fail."
"There is no place for me to belong."
"I am all alone."
"There's something wrong with me!"

These beliefs often arise out of early attachment injuries and traumas. They form when we don't get what we need—like emotional attention and support. They also form if we do get things we did not need—things that overwhelm us to a level that we cannot manage.

These negative stories are part of our primitive attempts to gain a sense of control over the overwhelm of such situations and to preserve the attachment relationships vital to our survival.

In the child's unconscious mind, it works similar to this:

"I am the bad one, you, the adult, are good.
When I change, I will be good again...
Then all will be well."

Of course, these negative assessments of self will not be conscious. Many of them originate before we develop complex language skills. Operating more as implicit beliefs, the child may not be able to articulate them directly in words.

Nevertheless, she will find herself drowning in these false negative beliefs, which if not corrected by an adult mind, will send her into a pit of darkness at some point in her life.

She needs an adult brain to help her unpack her negative beliefs and assign different meanings to her experience of *feeling bad*—so that she does not end up believing that she *is bad.*

Such unfortunate false beliefs often continue into adulthood and remain as implicitly stored negative assumptions about oneself and the world. In adulthood, she will find herself in stressful situations that resemble her unrepaired childhood wounds. These events will trigger the same sensations that were left unprocessed and unexplained.

Her implicit memory will then release the same sensory and emotional information, the knot in her stomach and pain in her heart. Her analytic left brain will automatically replay these false negative stories about herself and project negativity onto herself, the person in front of her, the situation, and even onto the future.

This is how the past leaks into and filters how we experience and view the present.

A child's brain will interpret things mostly in black-and-white, good vs bad, terms. A child has not developed sufficient brain capacity to hold shades of grey and the complexity of life. This is what an adult brain is capable of doing.

An adult brain has the capacity of holding complexity: good *and* bad, black *and* white, and all the shades of gray between. Even colors! However, adults can easily get triggered into falling back into more primitive modes of operation.

Under the spell of such primitive states, we will not be able to see how events are actually far more complex and nuanced than our simplistic, negative attributions.

We will keep ourselves attached to a negative story that our brains replay automatically. And our thoughts and feelings will be shaped by a simplistic albeit false storyline.

Meaning Making of Others

If we don't work through what drives such overly simplistic negative narratives about ourselves, then we will utilize other unhealthy strategies to deal with overwhelm. We will project these stories into the environment, and particularly onto people important to us—often our significant other.

The emotional power of unprocessed pain will color our interactions and the way we view not only ourselves but also others.

Especially when we are in distress.

Unprocessed emotions in the form of simplistic interpretations can be projected onto other people and situations in an attempt to finally find resolution to life-long insecurities and traumas.

As soon as we get into a meaningful relationship, whether it is through work, friendship, romantic or other, distress is inevitable. Of course, interpersonal distress does not depend on familiarity with the other person—it can happen any time we get distressed by our interactions with others.

Just consider how it can happen driving a car.

But when we have unresolved material from the past, any or all such stressors could trigger a survival response. Unaware of our own personal material we can easily end up acting out the unprocessed feelings from the past as if they are part of the situation that is happening now.

A client that I will call Isabelle, started therapy because she wanted to explore why she found herself in dangerous situations, wanting to rescue people at the expense of her own safety.

She reported that she felt extremely angry if she saw unfairness. I could certainly relate to having a sensitivity to unfairness. I could see that she deeply cared for injustice in the world, and often reflected on what she could do to help.

After some time in therapy, she stated that she also liked writing angry comments in social media. She wrote those comments whenever she perceived unfairness in order to protect and to stand up for the victim—even for people she did not know.

She said this gave her a huge sense of relief.

However, with one of the last angry comments she made online, she suddenly realized that she was being extremely unfair to the person she blamed.

She harshly blamed this person for giving up a job as a healthcare provider during the pandemic. But then, later, that same person revealed that she was diagnosed with stage 4 cancer.

The story Isabelle had was that this person was being extremely selfish for quitting her job in a time of extreme need.

Once she saw the person had metastatic cancer, she felt a deep sense of shame. This shame resulted in symptoms of depression, which she had a hard time to manage.

She said that she might have been unfair to others by blaming them, without giving any consideration to what they might have been going through.

She had the realization that she had become the very person she was trying to protect the victims from in the first place.

That made her want to stop and question what was driving her anger to the point of being unfair to others.

As we explored further, she was able to see how anger about childhood physical abuse still lived in her to this day. She had been heavily beaten by her uncle as a child, into her teenage years. She said she could not protect herself. She wished an adult would stand up for her which never happened.

In her first marriage, she could not feel a sense of safety as she anticipated her husband would also be violent towards her.

Earlier in her marriage she could never identify why she was so suspicious of him—which kept her in the dark, believing her negative thoughts and feelings about him. This especially was true if they argued and he got visibly upset.

Even though he never became physically abusive with her, his upset behaviors would get translated by her brain into her worst-case fear—which was that she didn't matter. As a couple they never questioned the ways their minds so often misinterpreted each other's upset behaviors, especially how those were fueled by each of their early unresolved emotions.

In most relationships, such false interpretations flow in both directions. Each partner sees the other through the lens of the unresolved past.

Her husband did not know how to relate to his pain. So he often misinterpreted her—believing that she didn't care about how he felt. This reflected his childhood dilemma of emotional neglect.

They often found themselves in arguments they could not manage effectively. As she would feel more anxious and angry, her husband felt more scared and depressed. Eventually they divorced.

If we are not aware of how our nervous system operates, we will unconsciously persuade ourselves that the person in front of us in the here and now fits the worst-case scenarios stored in memories of our distant past.

We will assign the "bad" evaluation to the other person in order to get a sense of control, so that we can finally protest and protect ourselves from the "bad" we experienced growing up. Protesting may be something we may never had been able to do in the past to the person we really needed to address.

For the non-analytical part of the brain time and space are irrelevant. Our system relives unprocessed sensations, feelings and thoughts over and over again if we don't pause to listen.

Isabelle's story demonstrates how someone who had been unfairly treated in the past unconsciously becomes the one who treats others unfairly.

We swap roles—if we were the victim once, we become the oppressor without knowing that we are repeating the cycle of trauma.

To me, this is a core dilemma of humanity. We still don't know how to deal with pain in a way that fosters personal or collective growth. We project our worst fears onto others. Believing the projections, we inflict onto others what we have suffered in the past. Looking at the history of humanity, you can see this pattern acted out throughout the centuries.

That is why I believe pausing and listening can be revolutionary. Practicing a different way of handling pain can create a pathway that could help you find new meanings in life. It could also model healthy emotional skills to others around you.

Having worked with people from many countries in the world, I can report that when it comes to the matters of the nervous system, in our reactions to overwhelm, pain or projection, and to the longings of the heart, we all speak the same language.

As infants, we all needed an adult caregiver to survive. We all were shocked as babies if neglected. We all can get angry in the face of unfairness. We all grieve loss.

Where we differ is how we choose to relate to our experience, especially when we are in pain.

The question is this…

How might we find new meaning through pain so that we don't have to hold it in our system forever while not turning into the very thing that hurt us in the first place?

Points to Keep in Mind

To summarize what we have discussed so far here is a list of things that can be important and useful to you to remember:

- Depression and anxiety are states of being stuck in high or low arousal. These states correspond to animal defense responses to threat, danger or overwhelm.

- The high arousal defenses are fight or flight. This also includes lock-up freeze, stuck like a deer in the headlights. The latter state results in anxiety, where the nervous system is highly aroused but overwhelmed and unable to move that strong energy in any productive direction.

- The low arousal defense is freeze or shut down in a numb or collapsed state. This is depression. It resembles being under the spell of anesthesia, not able to move, think, or feel.

- A common cause of these states of overwhelm is trauma. Hence, depression and anxiety can be seen as the inability to get out of animal survival responses to trauma.

- Either way, high or low arousal, life energy is stuck, buried in the musculature, in other parts of the body, and in the psyche. Such traumatic responses don't just impact our physiology. They also affect our heart and mind.

- This is where deep negative stories and beliefs arise. A child's survival depends on attachment to the adult caregiver. When attachment injuries occur, then to make meaning of these events and also preserve the attachment relationship, a child develops negative beliefs about the self.

- Those negative assumptions about the self will then turn into negative inner narratives that take the form of ongoing self-hatred, self-judgment, self-criticism, or harsh judgement and criticism directed to others.
- As adults, when we find ourselves in a state of distress that resembles a childhood experience,

our unprocessed feelings will restimulate these same negative stories and beliefs.

- The nervous system will be overwhelmed, and it will trigger defensive strategies similar to those used in childhood. Then we may fall into states of lock-up freeze or collapse, thus scare ourselves into anxiety or depression. What was once a useful survival strategy in childhood turns into an impediment to wellness in adulthood.

- It is always important to question the validity of the negative thoughts we hear inside our mind. These highly-distorted stories are automatically confabulated. And since they are unconsciously produced, we tend to believe them.

- But by starting to question such overly-simplistic internal narratives like *"there's something wrong with me"* we can reduce the unconscious power they have over us.

- If we become skeptical of those negative stories our mind tells us, we can engage in the process of inquiry—and develop more complex, nuanced, and compassionate inner narratives about ourselves and others. In doing this, we'll usually need to process deeper emotional layers from our past, to heal the roots of our fears.

- Whenever you hear your mind tell you a negative story, a powerful move is to pause and directly ask yourself, *"Is that really true?"* Can you open yourself up to the answer being *"No"*?

CHAPTER 3

AN ARTISTIC PERSPECTIVE

"Beni kör kuyularda merdivensiz bıraktın.
Denizler ortasında, bak yelkensiz bıraktın."
— ÜMIT YAŞAR OĞUZCAN

Fritz Perls, the founder of Gestalt Therapy, said the healthiest form of projection is art. Art offers an infinite space for projection and complex meaning making.

Ancient cultures utilized the arts to help process important, meaningful events such as birth, death, and various rites of passage.

Current art therapies were developed by artists and therapists who were deeply immersed in a form of artmaking. Discovering the potent medicine that can come out of the arts, they wanted to share it with the field of psychology.

Therapists indeed can learn much from artists.

They can learn to better utilize nonlinear forms of thinking, expression, and processing. Artists aim to translate invisible felt senses into tangible works of art. They might do this using sounds, words, movements, shapes or colors.

Through an artform, artists aim to make the invisible more visible in a way that creates beauty. The artwork can engage the viewer or listener and evoke deeper awareness.

Art inspires its audience.

It can also offer an experience of transformation to those who engage in the creative process. Such transformation arises from a process of self-inquiry and an intention to heal.

Artists can hold intense, challenging emotional material without judgment or overanalysis. They are able to bring empathy, a felt sense and intuition to the human experience—without diagnosing it.

Artists can offer presence to a difficult experience by engaging a heart-felt space. Therapists can learn from artists to engage more in the intuitive use of metaphors and symbols as a language of the soul.

Thus creative arts therapies access the medicinal power of creativity through forms of art-making.

Artists can learn much from therapists, too.

One thing they can learn is how being expressive can include titration and integration. Titration is a method used in chemistry—adding one solution into another slowly, one drop at a time. It is like eating one slice of bread one bite at a time rather than trying to swallow the whole loaf.

In current trauma therapy, a titrated approach to work with intense emotional material has proven to foster integrated change far better than the intensive cathartic approaches that were so common decades ago.

Artistic expression is often oriented to pushing back against constraints and being as dramatic and impactful as possible.

This parallels the 1970s period of humanistic psychotherapy, where catharsis and highly dramatic expression prevailed—and largely failed to serve in integrating the meaning and message of the feelings.

But that was then, and this is now.

Current psychotherapists usually understand the need for a titrated approach to healing. And this can provide structure and meaning to the transformative engagement found in artmaking.

Without the pressure of performing, being good or being liked, therapy offers a safe space where we can learn to explore depth in ourselves, away from the limelight, the image-making, the applause or the fear of harsh judgement—at least from the outside.

What therapy provides in combination with art-making is a space for healthy, productive meaning-making. In this space, the emotional and analytical approaches can meet and co-create transformative experiences, that will be integrated into healing.

Art is a powerful way of accessing the nonlinear, nonverbal material that often sits at the root of our personal suffering. Together with therapy, and respecting the need for titration, making art can offer us a way to name and put things into a better context and realign our internal experience.

The Arts in the Service of Healing

By consciously engaging in the creative process, we can intentionally use the arts in the service of healing. Rather than worrying about the success or impact of an art piece, we can spend time slowly digesting materials that emerge through sensations, metaphors and symbols.

Such a titrated approach allows time to digest potentially difficult emotional material in small quantities. It gives space for its meaning, story, and medicine to be revealed.

Ümit Yaşar Oğuzcan was one of the most prominent poets of Turkey. He struggled with mental health issues throughout his life and used poetry as an outlet for self-expression. At a very dark time in his life, when his son committed suicide, he wrote the lines I quoted at the beginning of this chapter.

Here is a translation from the Turkish:

"You left me in a blind well without a ladder.
You left me in the middle of the ocean
without a sail."

This famous poem also became the lyrics of a famous song composed by my grandfather. I sang this song in many concerts with my father. It continues to be sung to this day, bringing soothing relief and a sense of connection among people.

After losing his son, the poet Oğuzcan continued using poetry to process his pain. His poems became a gift to others who were similarly hurt.

There are many examples like this where artists around the world, have used art to process their personal pain. And long after their death their medicine continues to affect others who experience their artwork.

The arts provide a safe container to explore feelings and inner states while serving as a bridge for connection between our inner emotional state and our higher capacity to express and contain our feelings.

The arts provide a blank canvas, a clear page, an empty space in which there is possibility not only to contain but also to transform dark internal states.

In alchemy, this is referred to as "turning lead into gold." The alchemist, by applying fire, transforms a common substance into a precious metal. This takes place in the crucible, or the container into which the substance is put for this transformation.

In a similar way, depression is a lot like lead.

It is heavy, inert, and of little apparent value to those who possess it. The crucible can be an art-form—a container for exploring what is underneath the symptoms. The conscious intention to explore will light the flame. As we put our attention into our moment-to-moment experience, we will notice shifts and will have more resourceful access to ourselves.

What to Learn from Fear

Fear starts with a startle response. This is followed by orienting, which could evoke the actions of fight or flight. The aim of taking either action is survival. Anxiety can be seen as a lingering fear response from the past that has not yet been resolved. It keeps being projected into the future.

Anxiety is a common issue for performers. Stage fright involves the fear of failure, criticism, and judgement. This gets fueled by projecting these negative expectations into the future.

However, many performers also say that they need "the right amount of nervous energy" to meet an audience. Anxiety before a performance is like riding a wave. Once the wave breaks, productive energy is flowing. Connection to the audience is enlivened. The performance is energized and enriched.

Performers know that the energy fear provides is valuable. Without it a performance can be flat. There won't be sufficient energy to meet an audience.

Similarly, in life, fear can certainly be a signal to seek safety.

But it could also be an automatic response to a negative projection into the future. And we could automatically get derailed from taking appropriate action—even when the projection is coming from within us rather than actually being in the environment around us.

All too frequently people become disorganized or stuck due to imagined fears that are actually false projections of their past. So it can be quite valuable to learn to contain the energy that fear produces in our bodies and nervous systems.

Learning to contain a certain degree of the energy of fear could serve as fuel for us to take appropriate action.

As we repeat doing this, our nervous system can gradually learn to hold and channel more energy rather than react as if there is danger. This approach will lead us to increasingly be able to make use of the fuel that fear provides.

In the presence of ongoing anxiety, it is useful to inquire into the deeper layers that drive that hyper-aroused state.

Inquiring about what drives depression can also bring us into the depths of our psyche and offer rich personal emotional material. Once accessed, we can further give creative expression to this material in a way that also speaks to larger archetypal stories involving struggles of humanity at large.

With the right intention and approach, intense emotional states can be managed and expressed in a way that touches beauty. We can safely begin the journey of transforming our own material through the light of creativity.

In the remainder of this chapter, we will explore several different artforms as containers for transforming depression and anxiety.

First, we will look at music.

This will be followed by exploring theater, then movement, and finally drawing.

I have included exercises to help you experience from the inside out the concepts I present. The short ones can be done as you read the exercise. For the longer ones, I made audio recordings to guide you in case you prefer listening.

Music

Classical Turkish music has musical scales called *makam*. Each makam has a distinct quality of mood and scale.

In the 12th century Seljuk Empire mental illness was treated through the use of music. This treatment modality was expanded and continued during the Ottoman Empire starting in the 13th century.

Each makam was believed to have an effect on certain parts of the body. Makams could calm excessive activation, evoke peaceful states, and give voice to complex inner feelings.

Doctors especially were interested in the relationship between music and the heartbeat.

Music has an organizing effect on the brain.

Music can have a strong impact on how we feel and process our experiences. A simple example is the soundtrack of a movie that dramatically affects how the viewer responds to a particular scene.

When I worked at a psychiatric hospital I saw how the combination of melody, lyrics and rhythm helped patients organize their internal experience.

One patient having a hard time speaking could easily accompany lyrics. Another who had difficulty with balance and motion could calm down and get more organized upon hearing a steady beat. Patients with memory problems could remember the melody and lyrics of songs. I witnessed clinically depressed patients start to feel energized when they sang songs with others.

Our inner states are very much like makams. Each has different frequencies and varying modes of expression, similar to how these musical scales are organized.

When a makam meets poetry and tempo, a song is created. The way a makam couples with words and rhythm will deepen a certain mood. Or it can add another layer, a higher degree of complexity.

For instance, a sad makam may couple with sad lyrics and a slow tempo. When one hears the song, one may directly touch one's own sadness.

On the other hand, a song may have sad lyrics coupled with a brightly scaled makam as well as an upbeat tempo and rhythmic structures. The song may emanate a joyful, upbeat, or empowered mood. With closer attention to the lyrics, however, one may come to realize that this is also a song that deals with immense pain.

From a musician's perspective, depression and anxiety can be seen as certain makams playing within us at a specific tempo. If we are willing to cultivate the ear of a musician, we can learn to listen and even "play" the makams of anxiety or depression.

We can sing a melody or make sounds, tap the rhythms, and write the lyrics. We can even learn to switch to a different makam and rhythm. Doing this would enable us to start to feel different and develop a sense of agency—where we find effective ways to reorganize our internal experiences and feelings.

There are many pieces of music, from simple to complex, that give depth and meaning to pain.

When put into musical expression, painful inner states, including depression and anxiety, can create captivating melodies. Depression may have a song to sing, anxiety may have specific lyrics to write—or a beat to tap.

If we can give voice to such inner states, we will initiate a process of transforming the pain. We may even touch other people who are experiencing a similar pain.

That kind of consciously creative connection to pain evokes a shift—a shift that says to oneself:

"I am being held."
"I am larger than the depression or anxiety."

One reason why depression or anxiety symptoms last is that we fight with the symptoms without trying to understand the purpose they serve. We may feel annoyed or defeated because the same song keeps playing within us as if on a tape loop.

In one or another of the common expressions of depression, we may engage in self-judgement, self-hatred, or self-criticism in an attempt to try to resolve painful states.

We can become so overwhelmed that we will lose perspective about the choices we actually have. Perhaps all that the song really needs is a listening ear—our listening ear.

It needs to be heard for what it really is.

And then a new direction can emerge out of our willingness to hear it.

I performed music with my father for years. Before each concert, we planned our repertoire based on the mood and tempo of the songs.

If too many slow songs with heavy lyrics (low arousal) were played one after the other, the audience would twitch, cough, or simply get bored.

If there were too many fast songs (high arousal), the audience's capacity for paying attention would diminish as well.

So, in our concerts, we had to strike a balance between activation and calmness. That way there was fluidity, and we would not lose connection with the audience.

Inner work is similar.

You tune your instruments. You look at your repertoire. You notice the makams, scales and chords playing inside. You learn to allow yourself to hear the voice of anxiety or depression. You learn to play their tunes consciously.

By intentionally doing that, you can develop your capacity to manage the repertoire of your internal concert.

So, attend to your inner concert. If you notice the same song playing over and over, you do have a choice.

You don't have to accept the thought:

"Oh well, the violin keeps playing that same sad tune... and I can't do anything about it."

You *can*.

You can *pause*.

You can listen *again*.

You can play the tune *consciously*.

You can ask other orchestra members to *support* the violin.

You can even ask the percussionist to take a solo!

The real question is what gets in the way of you realizing that you *do* have a choice.

Think about that.

Once you allow yourself to really hear the tune of the violin, with time, your orchestra will develop a sense of flow. It may want to shift to a different tune all by itself or you may give a different score to the orchestra to play.

Inner psychological work is about cultivating the capacity to listen.

As we listen to the sounds and voices within us, we open possibility to give expression to their yearnings. We allow our inner concert to reveal itself to us.

For some of us, listening has never been safe. So we may need support for a while. We may need some "listening lessons".

By allowing ourselves to listen more deeply within, we foster our own inner reorganization and sense of harmony.

The message in your favorite song...

A dear friend of mine absolutely loved the aria *Una Furtiva Lagrima* by Gaetano Donizetti. The title translates as *"A Hidden Teardrop"*.

She particularly loved this title of the aria.

After years of listening to it, upon reflection, she realized that this song hinted at her own silent tears. This shows how music can communicate emotional messages that our intellectual minds miss.

- *Think of a song you really like.*
- *Pay attention to the lyrics.*
- *What is the message of this song?*
- *What might this song be reflecting about you?*

When We Speak, We Sing

A musical instrument with us all the time is our own voice. We "sing" whenever we speak. We tone when we make sounds like "mmmm, wow, aha, ha, iaaaa, oooh..." Singing, whether we do it speaking or through music, has a power to reveal and change our emotional state.

Many factors come into play when we use our voice: our breathing, rhythm, resonance, pitch, our words and lyrics, the imagery we use, and the somatic shifts we notice in our bodies. All these factors reflect the emotional state we are in along with the state of our nervous system.

Sound, especially our voice, has immense power in how we connect to ourselves and others. It was when I lost my voice for a couple days that I realized what an important instrument my voice was to connect with others as well as to feel safe.

I was on a plane to Turkey. Due to an illness, I had temporarily lost my voice. The person sitting next to me asked me if I was familiar with Istanbul. I nodded my head yes. They asked about how they could get to a certain location.

As I opened my mouth to talk I remembered that I had no voice. It was an odd moment. I didn't know how to communicate the information. Eventually I wrote down how they could get to the location. I wanted to apologize for not being able to make a sound. I also realized how scary it was not to have a voice. I felt very vulnerable without it.

Much more than words, tone of voice conveys emotional information to our system. As infants, the quality of our caregiver's vocal tone had a huge impact on our wellbeing. We felt safe through receiving our caregiver's soothing voice tone along with being held.

But if a caregiver's tone was harsh or scary, we would react with fear—maybe hold our breath, tighten our neck or belly, shut down our voice, or scream loudly.

If we were raised in an environment where feelings were suppressed or disguised, then we might be extra sensitive to voice tone. We may have had to train ourselves to hear the real emotional message and adapt accordingly.

We often naturally pick up and even start imitating the vocal expression styles and tones of voice of people close to us. For years, people would mistake me for my mother when I answered the phone at home.

Notice the melody in your voice when you are excited, angry, sad or serious. Does your voice sound like someone close to you? Does your voice remind you or other people around you of anyone else they know?

Many people's nervous systems were trained to constantly be alert to vocal cues, scanning like radar, because words could not be trusted when they grew up—or because a caregiver could suddenly get scary.

Many other people grew up having to pressure themselves to say "yes" when they really meant "no" but had no way to voice their boundaries. Sometimes they learned to stay silent or even say "no" to what they really needed.

By engaging in vocal awareness we can connect to the fascinating deeper vocal cues within us. We can discover how we respond to other people's vocal expressions. We can also see how we might still be putting pressure on ourselves to sound a certain way. And become aware of how certain tones in our voice impact us in a positive way.

Practicing different vocal tones...

Say the sentence "I am not significant" *out loud using each of the four vocal tones listed below. Repeat each three times and pause before moving to the next.*

- *Serious and whispering.*
- *Soft and smiling.*
- *Yelling as if announcing important news.*
- *Joking and whispering.*

Which tone did you enjoy the most and why?

Now say the sentence "I do matter" *using each of the four vocal tones above. Repeat each one three times and pause before moving to the next.*

Which one did you enjoy most and why?

Think about a vocal tone of someone you know that you find safe and pleasant.

What makes it feel safe?

And as you think about and hear in your mind this tone right now, what do you notice?

Breath

On a psychological level, breathwork is a powerful method for shifting emotional states.

When we are anxious, our breath becomes fast and shallow. Instead of filling our lungs with a full breath, we take in quick, short breaths. This causes us to hyperventilate which in turn decreases carbon dioxide levels in our blood.

To breathe optimally, it's helpful to notice what is happening in our diaphragm. This is a powerful muscle that separates the abdomen from the chest. It moves when we breathe.

When we breathe out using our diaphragm and other muscles in the torso, we can make a prolonged sound.

The diaphragm regulates our ability to take in and to let out. When the diaphragm is tight, this impacts our ability to breathe in and out in a relaxed way. Over time this can have an emotional as well as a behavioral impact.

In a chain reaction to a tight diaphragm, neck, jaw and spine muscles tighten, and it takes far more effort to make sound. This could negatively affect our emotional state along with the sound and quality of our communication.

Noticing the movement of their ribs, singers practice expanding their lung capacity and abdominal space, including their back. They seek to balance relaxation with the right amount of energy, so that they can support a full musical phrase.

When the breath can be noticed to move the belly, the sides of the ribs, and even the back, there is more breathing space and support available to the singer.

This also impacts emotional states.

Like the singer, we all can benefit from noticing how our ribs, belly and back move as we inhale and exhale. Singing is music made on long out-breaths followed by easy inhales.

Furthermore, breath can help us settle into our experience deeper. In the audio recordings you may hear me breathe deeply as I describe an exercise. This is a habit I acquired in my training as a performer. By breathing deeply into my experiences, I was able to connect to myself and others—which as a performer enhanced my delivery and sense of flow.

We know that long exhales have a calming effect on the nervous system. Breathing deeply with long exhales calms and grounds us.

When we sing even a single note on a vowel, we invite more regulation into our system.

Pausing and feeling your breath...

- *Lie down and notice your breathing.*
- *Put your hand on your belly and notice if there is any movement there with each breath in and out.*
- *Then as you breathe out keep your belly out and don't let it sink until the last moment.*
- *When the exhale is complete, allow a new breath to come in on its own.*
- *Repeat this a few times.*
- *Then add sound on the outbreath by vocalizing a simple vowel, like* "aah" *or* "ooh"...

Resonance

Resonance is the quality of sound being full and rich due to being physically amplified. For instance, a guitar string gets plucked, and the vibrations get amplified by the body of the guitar. The guitar would not sound as rich or full if it did not have a resonant body to amplify the vibrations of its strings.

In singing and speech, the tones generated by our vocal chords will naturally resonate through cavities in our chest, mouth, throat and nasal passages. These cavities, some of which we can actively shape, amplify and enhance the sound coming out of our mouth.

You can become more aware of the spaces inside of you and explore vocal resonance. On a body level, exploring space within yourself and increasing your awareness of resonance can have emotional affects.

Both depression and anxiety include a sense of helplessness. We can feel a lack of inner and external resources. We may feel stuck in a particular negative feeling or thought pattern.

However, by noticing and spending time in your internal spaces that are available to you and by noticing the resonance of your own voice the message you are giving to yourself is very different from being stuck in one place.

If you explore your internal spaces—your throat, chest, nasal cavities, mouth—by making sounds that resonate in those spaces, you are literally moving through your internal landscape.

Exploring how your voice resonates differently through the different resonant spaces in your body offers you an opportunity to choose to experience how sound can flow inside you.

By noticing and spending time in your internal spaces that are available to you, and by noticing the resonance of your own voice—the message you are giving to yourself is of movement and flow.

Since everything in the body is interconnected, then as you notice how sound can flow, this could also start to move more of a sense of flow in your mental and emotional systems. You might even feel this directly in your body.

Exploring how sound resonates in you...

To listen to me guide you through this exercise in an online audio, use this link:

hazalselcuk.com/tunnel-exercises

Or you can just do the exercise as you read the following page.

- *Lie down and start to notice each of your in-breaths and out-breaths.*
- *Notice how your torso moves with each breath you take in and let out.*
- *As you breathe out, shape the vowel* "ooh" *with your mouth—but without making any sound.*
- *Do this a few times.*
- *Put one hand on your chest.*
- *Next, breathe out and tone* "ooh" *a few times, noticing any vibration you feel in your chest.*
- *Move your hand to wherever you feel this vibration.*
- *Do the same thing using a lower tone.*
- *Do you notice more or less vibrations?*
- *Continue doing this for a full minute.*
- *Vary the tones you make and track where you feel the vibrations.*
- *Now just rest and notice whatever you are experiencing inside.*
- *Next, as you exhale, sound a higher note with the tone* "eee".

- *Do this again and sense wherever this tone vibrates in your body.*
- *Repeat* "eee" *a few more times and notice.*
- *Gently touch the area where you feel the vibration the most.*
- *Rest for a moment and notice what that was like for you.*
- *Reflect on which tone better matched your inner state at this moment. Was it the low* "ooh" *or the high* "eee"*?*
- *Continue toning it now if you enjoyed any particular tone.*

The field of sound healing holds that everything naturally vibrates at its own resonant frequency. And when vibrating at that frequency, it releases energy. Furthermore, it states that each of us has a unique resonant frequency. And when we meet ourselves at that frequency, energy gets released.

As depression and anxiety can be seen as being stuck in an unhealthy energetic state, setting our life energy free to move again is particularly important. So in that regard, what does "meeting" ourselves at our resonant frequency mean?

On a physical level, the exercise above is about detecting and tracking how different frequencies of sound you produce vibrate and resonate at differing locations in your body.

As you explore this, you get more self-aware of what is energetically taking place within you. In other words, you are tuning into yourself.

We could call this an act of "self-attunement."

Self-attunement means meeting ourselves where we are in the moment—emotionally, mentally and physically. Doing this enables us to enter the here and now—the only place in time where transformation is truly possible. Rather than ignoring or resisting what is going on inside of us, we move towards it, explore it, and tune into it.

Think of this as similar to how a musician tunes an instrument. The goal is to make it sound better. But the act of tuning starts with slowing down and really hearing the sound coming out of that instrument in the present moment.

By noticing which spaces in your body resonate with sound you can give voice to whatever you are experiencing in the here and now. You then start to explore and attune to the most basic instrument of all—the human voice.

You could explore "singing" your thoughts and feelings by working with consonants or even words. You could also explore toning a desired energetic state. For example, what would be the vowel and tone for the state of feeling calm. What about for joy?

Giving voice to self-attunement...

To listen to me guide you through this exercise in an online audio, use this link:

hazalselcuk.com/tunnel-exercises

Or you can do the exercise reading the following.

- *Please take a moment to tune into wherever your emotional and energetic states are.*
- *From this place, start toning a vowel you want to explore. It could be "ooh", "eee", "aah" or any other vowel you wish.*
- *Tone this vowel a couple more times.*
- *Now tone it more quietly a few times.*
- *Notice what happens to your energy state. Does it change in any way?*
- *Next, tone it more loudly a few times.*
- *Notice what happens to your state.*
- *Tone it in the volume that feels just right to you.*
- *Find an unpleasant thought and sound it using a stream of consonants. Like "kk", "ch", "ff", "tt" or any others that come to mind.*

- *Turn up the volume of this stream.*
- *Turn down the volume.*
- *Now find the volume that is most fun to you.*
- *Finally, choose an energetic state you would like for yourself. It could be peace, calm, joy, acceptance, or any other state you wish.*
- *Explore and find a vowel you can tone that feels best to match that state.*
- *Tone this vowel a couple more times.*
- *Play with the volume to get it the best for you.*
- *Now just rest.*
- *What do you notice? What feels different?*
- *Stay with it.*

Tempo and Rhythm

Tempo is a term that relates to the speed of music, from fast to slow. *Rhythm* is the timing of when notes occur in relationship to each other.

Legato is a musical term that describes how the notes get played, wherein each note connects to the next. *Staccato* is a term that indicates a series of short notes, often detached from one another.

Both the rhythmic structure and tempo of a song affects our physiology and moves us into a particular state or mood. In many cultural traditions chanting and repetition of a certain rhythm is used to create a desired emotional state.

In speaking, depending on our mood, our speech will carry a certain rhythm. This shows up through how slow or fast we speak and how long we pause. Our overall tempo can be fast or slow, and our words can be legato or staccato, or a combination of both. Short or long pauses may also be interspersed.

Depression has a slow tempo and slow rhythm. So does a calm state. Anxiety has a fast tempo and fast rhythmic structures. So does excitement. When we speak, our tempo varies with our emotional state, as reflected in our nervous system's level of activation vs relaxation.

Consciously exploring your own tempo gives you valuable information about yourself. It may affect your feelings as well as those of the listener.

For instance, if you intentionally slow down your speech, it can strengthen your ability to convey a message and increase the ability of the other person to receive it.

Slowing down can feel uncomfortable at first if you are used to living life at a quick tempo. However, thoughts run at a much faster tempo than the body or emotions do. To get a better grasp of our internal state, we must slow down, or even pause to catch up with aspects of ourselves. Then, we can make more informed choices and honor our deeper parts.

For many of us, slowing down does not feel safe. So we unconsciously speed up to avoid feeling our depths. To slow down feels uncomfortable and we just keep jumping from one thing to the next.

Tempo and rhythm are the heartbeat of how we relate to life, to other people, and to ourselves. It can be worth observing how fast your "life beat" is and reflect if you are moving at the speed at which you really want to go through life.

Sensing your tempo and rhythm...

What do you sense about your speed right now. Fast or slow? Are you content with it? Do you want to slow down or speed up?

- *Say this:* "I am breathing in and out."
- *Repeat this several times.*
- *Sense your tempo.*
- *Then speed up as you say it few more times.*
- *And then say it slowly a few times.*
- *Finally, say it at the tempo that is the most comfortable for you.*

Pitch and Intensity

Pitch refers to how high or low the frequency of a note is. On a piano, low notes are on the left end of the keyboard and high notes are on the right. As you move from left to right, the strings get shorter so the frequency of their vibration gets higher.

Loudness is how strong a note sounds and this correlates to that note's energetic intensity. If you strike a piano note strongly, this will make the string vibrate more energetically, and so it sounds louder. Press a key softly, and the note will sound soft.

Pitch can go hand-in-hand with loudness, but not always. For instance, a tuba can play a low note very loudly. Or a violin can play a very high-pitched harmonic softly.

In both singing and speaking, pitch and loudness will continually vary. These nonverbal factors convey emotional information about the state of a speaker or the mood of a song.

The pitch and loudness—in addition to tempo—might be calming, exciting, comforting, anxiety provoking or depressing. Imagine singing a lullaby at a very high pitch. Depending on the quality of your voice and how loud it is, it may scare the infant.

Animals are highly sensitive to pitch and intensity. We humans are, too. In communication, the pitch and intensity, far more than the words, convey emotional states and meaning.

In general, the "music of anxiety" is higher in pitch, faster in tempo, and louder in intensity. By contrast, the "sound of depression" is lower, slower, and softer.

When you start to listen to your own voice, you can begin to bring awareness to how internal states might be expressing themselves through your pitch and intensity as well as speed.

This can give you a clue about how your tone continues to affect you, and how it might impact the people around you. You could also start to recognize subtle pitch and loudness cues you might be sensitive to in your environment.

Playing with pitch and intensity...

- *Think of a lullaby or a familiar children's song. Pick any simple tune you know.*
- *Sing it out loud once.*
- *As you sang this tune, what happened to your energy level—did it get more activated or calmed?*
- *Next, sing it at a different pitch and intensity that is not at all appropriate for this tune.*

- *What happened for you when you did this? (Some people laugh, some get uncomfortable, some have fun with it.)*
- *What happens to your pitch and intensity when you get very angry?*
- *What happens to your pitch and intensity when you are sad?*
- *Now sing this tune once again in answer to this question: "What is the opposite pitch and intensity of anxiety—or depression?"*

Increasing awareness of your vocal output will enable you to strengthen your ability to notice your energetic level of being activated vs calm. Then when you do notice that your activation level is amped up, you could choose to pause and help yourself.

If you do notice this and pause, doing so can give you an opportunity to be curious about whatever it is that you really need in the moment. Do you want to speak more clearly? More calmly?

You could practice doing this as a tool to help yourself to better listen and follow where your inner states want to guide you. At the same time it would also be a way to increase your ability to communicate more consciously and effectively.

Words

Words have a profound impact. People can say certain things to us that will stick in our memories for decades. These could have been words that elevated us—or crushed us.

Whether talking to ourselves or with others, the words we use create an emotional atmosphere. They impact the quality of the "air we breathe" and "water we drink" in our internal environment, as well as in our relationships with others.

We can learn much from looking at how words and music combine in singing. The combination of melody and lyrics in a song conveys complex emotional information.

Many songs are composed using poetry. Poetry and music when combined can reach the depths of our humanity and give meaning to the most painful experiences like death and loss.

Words and music can hold complex emotional material and convey it artistically. Composed lyrics can create a space for connection, complexity, depth and harmony.

Because words and music can elevate very dark, deep, heavy emotional states in a masterful way, songs can help us tolerate and even transform pain and feel our finest human potential regardless of culture, age, gender, wealth or status. Songs can have the power to lead us to our humanness.

We use words combined with rhythm, pitch and intensity to communicate with others daily. And our words can be piercing, soothing, hurtful, encouraging or be taken in many other ways not only by those around us but also by our self.

Becoming more conscious of our use of words, along with nonverbal musical factors, will increase our connection within ourselves. Doing this internal work will open a different space for communication both within us and with other people.

 ***Reflecting on how you talk to yourself...***

Take a moment and consider this question: What kinds of words do you say to yourself when you are experiencing the symptoms of depression or anxiety?

Theater

Theater builds upon interpersonal dynamics. It gives shape to behaviors and relationships. It plays with tension, dramatizes conflict, delights with humor, and heightens feelings. It can display and intensify a wide range of expression, from subtle moods to explosive catharses.

Through the actor, we witness and vicariously experience emotional states. We view the unfolding of feelings in stages, from beginning to escalation and resolution.

Let's say we watch a character on stage grow from childhood to adulthood. At some point we see her struggle with depression. Through the course of the play we understand why. We hear her voice, see her body language, as we have emotional and somatic responses to this as an observer.

Through witnessing her verbal and nonverbal expressions, we have opinions about her, we feel for her, we intuit what she is longing for, we comment on her state. As we observe, we can access our own feelings and thoughts. We can deepen our sense of knowing what she needs to heal and grow.

Theater is a mirror for the actor and for the audience. It is a laboratory where we can let the darkness speak, evolve, and transform. Theater provides the freedom to be big, small, silly, depressed, angry, anxious, sad, to make sound, or to remain silent.

It is a place where attention gets directed consciously. Theater is life lived consciously for a few hours. We experience time as it expands and contracts and maybe also stops.

Inner Archetypes

Theater employs many metaphors and images connecting us to archetypes that carry emotional and psychic power. Archetypes are often used in myths and storytelling across different cultures. They portray universal character types and behaviors.

Archetypes live in us as resonances of the human experience. They represent characteristics that parts of us can relate to—the judge, the healer, the mother, the king, the fool, the evangelist, the skeptic, the teacher, the adventurer.

When we give voice to whatever archetypal quality wants to speak through us, this awakens an aspect of our life force that may have been dormant or previously inaccessible.

Through the lens of archetypes, depression can be seen as a character who has a story to tell and a message to deliver. If we learn to listen to its story, and embody its character consciously, we create space to receive its message. Dialogue with that part of the self will deepen connection, create self-awareness, and foster energetic flowing and healing.

Often, due to the lack of having experienced a healthy emotional environment growing up, we end up with fear that our "dark inner states" will be overwhelming. Therefore, we might unconsciously avoid and push these states away.

It is important to realize this fear comes from our childhood experiences. It is being projected into our lives today by memories from the past. But as adults, we don't have to be limited by this.

Expanding our capacity to be with our self will include learning to manage difficult inner states. By consciously giving voice to our inner states through the processes found in theatrical play, we can begin to create more flow between them.

Using your body, voice, movement, breath, or words, it becomes possible to experience a sense of control which then allows you to better embrace your nature and accept what is.

Theatrical play opens a stage for the expression of your whole psyche, without discrimination, prejudice or judgement. As diverse voices get heard, more unity is found within.

Caveflowers

Years ago I created a solo performance piece called *Caveflowers*. In it I explored the power of metaphors to work with depression. I used the metaphor of gardening to describe the healing process of a depressed woman who always wanted to sleep.

The woman complained that her backyard was not flowering no matter how much she watered her seeds. She was about to give up on herself. She kept saying that she didn't want to do anything other than just to sleep.

One day she heard someone breathing and talking. The voice came from under the soil in her backyard.

Anxiously, she started digging and eventually found a character who had been living under the soil for many years.

That character's name was "Sediment."

Hearing the woman digging into the soil, Sediment at first dug down even deeper into the earth to escape the shame of being seen with her deficiencies.

As we follow Sediment, we encounter other characters who all lived in hiding underneath the earth in caves…

There was a battered Middle Eastern woman from the countryside who wanted to commit suicide.

There was an angry man who had been beaten and tortured.

There was an old woman who was neglected as a baby because she was a girl.

And there was an elderly man who lost his children in war and could no longer feel he was good enough.

All these characters were very thirsty.

But there was an owl that controlled the water supply. The owl refused to give any water to anyone.

There was also a character called "Flower Woman".

Flower Woman drummed and sang. She could go in and out of the caves under the soil, or she could be above ground conversing with other humans. She brought movement, sound, energy, power and empathy into the world and to the underworld.

Flower Woman carried seeds which were sprinkled about at the conclusion of each dance.

Some seeds fell into the caves.

With the help of Flower Woman, Sediment managed to defeat the owl and give water to the seeds.

These seeds eventually began to sprout.

Hence, the flowers became "Caveflowers".

As I was preparing this performance piece, I could feel a big shift in my own psyche. Flower Woman had planted a seed in me which later sprouted as I became a therapist.

After the completion of that play, I never experienced a lasting stuck state of depression again. Still to this day, when I feel a bit depressed, I treat it as my soul wanting to communicate an important message to me.

I ground myself into presence and listen.

I allow myself to not feel good.

There is so much pressure in our world to "be on," "feel good," and "be great" all the time.

It is as if we just want it to be summer all year around—where it is always sunny, never cloudy.

But rainy days can be calming if you have an umbrella, the right coat, and a project to work on. Snow can also be beautiful with its silent, peaceful white cover, if you have a cozy home and a warm blanket.

Our work is to make the umbrella, the home, and the warm blanket accessible to our psyche.

The archetypes inside of you...

- *What archetypes are you aware of operating inside of you?*
- *Which one is the most interesting to you?*
- *How does this archetype express itself in you?*
- *What is it like for you to get in touch with this particular archetype?*

Movement

Life is movement. It is energy in motion.

And movement generates power.

In nature, we can see this in both obvious and subtle forms—from the dramatic power of ocean waves crashing against shoreline rocks to succulents quietly forming intricate spiral patterns of geometrical movement as they slowly grow.

Trees encompass many patterns of energy. Branches reach out into space in unique curves, spirals, and bends. A squirrel runs and jumps along the branches like a circus performer. Water flows up and down inside the trunk of the tree. Light enters the leaves and turns them red in the fall. As a seed sprouts, eventually to become a tree, we can see energy and movement playing out over time.

In a depressed state, it seems like life energy has been frozen and our motivation for movement has stopped. Thus, it becomes difficult to access movement. Our lack of movement further reinforces a sense of blockage and powerlessness.

In an anxious state there is excessive activation, but the energy has no clear direction. It lacks organization. So, it cannot reach a state of completion. It is like big waves not knowing where to flow. Without direction, their intensity keeps building. The waves get bigger unable to land on shore.

In the nervous system this results in a state of overwhelm and panic.

Peter Levine, in his book *Waking the Tiger,* presents the concept of a trauma vortex, which itself gives rise to a complementary entity called the healing vortex. These two interrelated vortices exist side by side. In the face of trauma, a healing vortex, which is the antidote to trauma, can be tapped into.

When effectively evoked, the healing vortex will speed up the steps to recovery in therapy. Thus, there is another side to depression or anxiety, that if we can access it, will lead us towards healing and wholeness.

Levine uses the metaphor of a river to describe how a healing vortex is intrinsically formed as a counter-vortex that balances the force of the trauma vortex.

When there is a rupture in the boundaries of a river, water overflows, swirling over the riverbank. This is the trauma vortex, a result of experiences that overwhelm and rupture what the boundaries of our psyche is capable of holding.

Levine states that a counter-vortex is simultaneously created, swirling water in the opposite direction back into the river. When we can recognize and utilize this healing vortex, we can move back into a coherent experience of the stream of life.

Seen through this lens, when we are experiencing depression or anxiety, it would be useful to redirect our attention for a moment towards the other side—where the healing vortex could be found and felt as a healing force.

When anxious, it might be possible to redirect my attention to a sense of being held by the floor, so that I can feel that I am being supported by gravity. I may also choose to notice how I am being held by the chair, how it is holding and supporting the weight of my body.

From that place, I can begin to tap even a little into the healing vortex, my inner resources to tolerate anxiety. The movement within my nervous system and body may then start to shift in a more coherent direction.

As I follow this direction, I may start to experience physical movements that further release activation. This may also have emotional significance. Continuing to stay with the energetic flow in my body, I may reach the other shore and recover a sense of deeper connectedness and calmness.

Or, I may choose to explore what is driving the anxiety in me. I may get curious about the subtle but powerful emotional dynamics that are sitting at the root of the anxious state.

In a depressed state, where motivation for motion seems to be blocked, I could first acknowledge what might still be moving in me all by itself.

Even in a depressed state, my blood still moves through my veins, my heart still is beating, my lungs are expanding and contracting with each breath. Cells are taking in nourishment, lymph nodes are filtering; my kidneys, liver, and stomach are in cycles of movement.

The inner intelligence of our being is always engaged in constant flow of movement and rest. Paying attention to this, I can tune into any form of movement in my body, perhaps followed by some rest.

I can begin by sensing micro-movements that are noticeable in me. Through further somatic and emotional inquiry I can slowly, in my own timing, begin a process of unwinding some patterns both in my physiology and my psyche.

If there is enough movement and I have access to an alive stillness within me, I won't even notice what is going on in the depth of my bodily functioning. But if something is off balance, then I may notice how my natural flow is disrupted.

Often pain is an indicator that something is out of balance and that we need to give some attention and support to what is going on inside.

When one's nervous system is not experiencing threat, one is in a calm, safe state. Moshe Feldenkreis wrote that we must be helped to get to a state where we have a good nervous system, but do not need to know that we have a good nervous system.

The not knowing refers to a state of harmony and flow. There is nothing excessive or out of balance. It is as if the nervous system is not there, because it is operating as it should in the background.

Seen through this lens, depression and anxiety can be viewed as signals asking for your conscious attention. These are signals that our system has been overwhelmed, that we have excess or stuck energy, that we need to return to a state of better balance and a sense of flow. Movement and bodywork can be excellent portals for inquiry and guidance.

Through conscious inquiry, movement, stillness, and by giving attention to impulses in your body, in its own time a stuck state of overwhelm or freeze can dissolve. You can regain access to your life energy in a manner that brings you more grounding, flow and direction.

Mind-Directed Movement

Movement can happen in two different ways—*mind-directed* or *body-directed.*

Mind-directed movement is voluntary. It is consciously controlled, a result of us deciding to move a certain way. A simple example is that you choose to raise your right hand and you volitionally do so.

We can decide to engage in movement, even when it feels hard or if we don't feel like moving. For example, regardless of how we initially feel, we could choose to go out for a walk or swim or work out. We could decide to do some gardening, wash the dishes, or clean the house. Yet another way would be to take a dance class, a martial arts class, or a spin class.

We might even explore something new, like taking a Feldenkreis class—where we track our inner experience of doing a simple movement and notice the effect throughout our body. Certain approaches to movement, like Feldenkreis or Alexander work, can also foster inner stillness, awareness, and a sense of grounding, along with physical, emotional and mental flow.

Mind-directed movement involves doing or learning a specific way of moving and being able to repeat it. You direct your body to move in a certain way for a certain period of time. This form of movement can be very effective in the treatment of depression and anxiety.

In fact, research shows that in mild to moderate depression, exercise is as effective as antidepressants with the benefit of healthy side effects. Given that the motivation for movement is blocked in the collapsed state, one can *decide* to move even when one *doesn't feel* like it.

By directing oneself to move, one is inducing the body and brain to create positive chemistry of "feeling good" that movement produces. When repeated often enough, this will build a new habit and foster positive shifts overall.

That is why it can be valuable and important not to give into "not wanting to move" but instead take ourselves out for a walk, even if just for 10 minutes.

Taking a movement break...

To hear me guide you through this exercise, use this link: **hazalselcuk.com/tunnel-exercises**

Or just do the exercise as you read the following...

- *Check in with your body right now.*
- *Where do you feel relaxed? Where are you tense?*
- *What part of your body feels most alive in this moment? Or asleep?*
- *Where are you at emotionally?*
- *Mentally?*
- *Now take a moment and look at your hands.*
- *Move your fingers.*
- *Now make five circles with your wrists.*
- *Wiggle your toes—close and open them five times.*
- *For one minute move your hands, arms, legs and feet in any way you wish.*
- *You can shake your arms and legs.*
- *See if you have any impulse to stretch, yawn, or to do anything else, and just do that. You can get up and use the whole space.*

- *Now reach out with your arms.*
- *Lower them.*
- *Reach up to the sky.*
- *Then bring your arms down.*
- *Open your arms to the sides.*
- *Reach all the way up.*
- *Slowly bend your elbows.*
- *Then let your arms fall.*
- *Shake off your torso.*
- *Rest.*
- *Again, open your arms to the sides.*
- *Reach all the way up.*
- *Slowly bend your elbows.*
- *Then let your arms fall.*
- *And shake off your torso.*
- *Check in with your body again.*
- *Where are you open, and where are you tense?*
- *Scan within yourself for a part of your body that feels the most alive in this moment.*
- *Where are you at emotionally?*
- *Mentally?*

Body-Directed Movement

The other form of movement is body-directed. That is, we allow our body itself decide how it will move. Here's a simple example. We direct our attention to track our bodily sensations. We might then notice that our upper body has tightened and our shoulders have raised a bit all by themselves.

We won't know beforehand what any particular movement will be. Letting our body move when it wants to and how it wants to, we simply track and follow the impulses that arise from within.

The body does what it wants to do. It could yawn, stretch, turn away, turn to the side, to the back. It may twitch, shake, make movements towards closing, opening, reaching, pushing, grasping, kicking, or anything else.

Our conscious mind follows the body's impulses and does not try to direct or control the movement. As this type of involuntary movement happens, we allow the body to find its own way of moving. We don't try to analyze, interpret, or make up any story about what the movement "means."

In some forms of movement practice—Authentic Movement for example—participants take turns in small groups being a mover or witnessing the mover. At the end each person discusses their experiences as the mover or witness.

This conversation can be verbal or conducted through movement alone. The processing allows the mover to receive feedback about how their movement impacted the witnesses.

The witnesses engage in an active sensing process as they observe the mover. They notice and share any relevant personal material that was brought up by the mover.

Body-directed movement allows the body to tell its own story through sensations, impulses followed by movement, and images. It enables the body to have a dialogue with the mover's personal psychological material while naturally opening up space for flow.

From this place one may experience images or metaphors that offer strong messages.

Such somatic movement practices activate and strengthen kinesthetic, proprioceptive awareness (feeling the body from the inside and following its impulses). They facilitate the access to wisdom of the body, wisdom that offers a particular medicine.

This medicine can be a set of movements, sounds, words, images, physical actions, stillness, or anything else that may have a strong psychological resonance.

Movement practices—body-directed or mind-directed—can be deeply healing. They can help us reconnect within ourselves and begin to experience a sense of inner flow, strength, flexibility, balance, and self-expression.

Drawing

One of the most effective ways to explore your physical and emotional landscape is by drawing. I am not good at realistic drawing, so when I engage in a drawing activity I call it "playing with colors in movement."

I allow the impulses in my hands to make shapes on the paper as I chose the colors I feel attracted to. After some time, the drawing starts speaking to me, and I engage in a dialogue through colors and shapes.

Drawing is a wonderful way to "get rid of distress" while at the same time creating a safe distance to feel into the distress and have a dialogue with it.

The drawing paper takes the distress onto itself and helps you to relate to it by playing with it visually. In this form of aesthetic engagement, one slows down and starts to see a problem from a different perspective.

The problem is being held by the artwork. This helps you more clearly see it, relate to it, and even play with it nonverbally, through colors, shapes, and images. As you play with it, you can witness the piece transforming in front of your eyes.

As you further engage with the aesthetic confrontation and play, you continue making decisions in each moment. Those are aesthetic decision each of which can have a resonance in your internal landscape.

The shifts you see happening in front of your eyes may echo within you as you allow yourself to be with the evolving piece. You decide the colors, size, shapes and images. This process can be rich and complex and have immense therapeutic value.

By engaging in an activity like drawing, you start to get interested in how distress gets represented on paper. In this creative process there is room for new information to emerge. You can discover alternative ways to relate to an old issue. Instead of trying to get rid of it, you get engaged in portraying the depression in an aesthetic form.

If depression or anxiety is the smoke, then artistic inquiry gives us new, useful information about the fire. Engaging with our inner states on an aesthetic, metaphorical basis creates a level of distance and interest that facilitates us to lend our heart safely to the cry of the depression or anxiety.

Drawing Your Feelings...

- *Draw your current emotional state.*
- *Play with different colors and shapes.*
- *Next, draw a state that would be the opposite.*
- *Rest.*
- *Notice any shift in your experience of yourself.*

Imagination

Using our imagination is often the first step to making things happen. We first see it in our minds, then manifest it in the world. The power of imagination has long been used in the arts. Some pianists practice as much with an imagined "keyboard" in their mind as they do with a physical keyboard.

Creativity is all about imagination.

We might hear a melody in our mind before we play or sing it. We could internally see some scene or image before we paint it on a canvas. We may first imagine characters and their dialogues and then start writing a play, a novel or a poem.

We give shape to thoughts, feelings, and internal sensations through imagination. When we speak, we have images in our minds to which we associate our words. These images can be positive or hurtful.

We imagine when we listen to music and when we read poetry. When we hear someone's voice or read their writing, we imagine how they might look or feel. When we meet someone new, we imagine a potential friendship, a work, a romantic or an artistic partnership. We might automatically imagine scenes we may want to move towards or scenes we want to run away from.

What we find ourselves imagining vs what we want to imagine can give us important information about the deeper emotional dynamics that reside and play out within us.

Through vocal toning, singing, writing, drawing, music making and movement we can develop our internal imagery and consciously notice the impact it has on us.

Imagining...

- *If you let yourself just imagine for a moment, what is the first thing that comes to mind?*
- *Allow yourself to daydream or just imagine anything that has a positive feel to you. What happens?*
- *How is for you it to allow yourself to imagine that particular dream?*

Finding the Beauty

Whether it is through music, theater, movement, drawing, poetry, or any other artform, the intention of artistic expression and inquiry is to be with whatever is. It is a form of offering unconditional love to oneself. We can do this in an aesthetic manner. We can engage with depression or anxiety and get to the beauty of it.

This may initially sound very odd to you: the *beauty* of depression and anxiety. How can depression or anxiety turn into something beautiful?

What could that beauty possibly be?

That beauty is our *vulnerability* expressed in artistic form, whether a piece of music, dance, painting, poetry, writing or theater. It is our hearts opening up even just a little bit, even for a few seconds.

And it is not just *our* vulnerability, but really when we look deeper, we realize that we are getting in touch with the vulnerability in all humans, the vulnerability of humanity itself.

In the light of all that we discussed so far here are some questions you might want to consider and see what answers emerge. I suggest asking a question and then just waiting for an answer to find you—rather than pressuring yourself to come up with what you think the answer should be.

I recommend you take some time with each of these questions and really feel into each one.

You could take a day or even a week for each question.

And do remember, let the answer find you...

- *What might depression want to tell you?*
- *What might anxiety be trying to protect you from?*
- *What is depression's song lyrics, anxiety's monologue, dance, shape, or colors?*
- *If depression or anxiety were a character in a movie, how would it look, how would it move and talk?*
- *When you experience symptoms of anxiety or depression how do you talk to yourself? What is the tone and volume of your inner voice?*

These questions and more could be explored by engaging in artistic and creative processes that foster inquiry and embodiment.

The arts offer us a rich container for nonlinear inquiry and expression. By engaging in a creative exploration of an emotional issue, you can tap into forms of self-expression in which metaphors and symbols can speak through sounds, words, shapes, colors, characters or movement.

And to repeat what I often tell my clients, you don't have to be an "artist" to benefit from engaging in any of these artistic activities.

You are not doing it to perform for anyone.

You are not doing it to entertain anyone.

There is no art critic involved.

There's not even an audience.

You are doing it to evoke and experience the kind of profound inner knowing that you can tap into when you engage the creative process.

Often, such inner knowing is the very medicine we need.

This medicine is very different than a pill prescribed by a doctor or psychiatrist.

This medicine is prescribed by your own healing vortex—by your soul delivered through engaging in the language of the arts.

For your listening & viewing pleasure...

I would like to share with you a music video that shows how I personally used some of the ideas we have discussed in this chapter to explore grief.

Access the video by using this link:

hazalselcuk.com/tunnel-exercises

This is only meant to inspire you, not to set up a standard to aim for. The intention of our work here has nothing to do with professional music production or performing for an audience.

If you would like to see more of my music videos, you can find my YouTube channel here:

youtube.com/channel/UC7p73A0nO5eQaX6gFECVSLA

CHAPTER 4

ATTENTION, INTENTION & INQUIRY

"Attention, intention, and inquiry have given me a sense of organization to the chaos within."
— SAID BY A PATIENT IN A PSYCHIATRIC HOSPITAL

The direction of our attention can be outward into the world. It can also be inward, into ourselves. Or it can encompass both directions. Whatever we put our attention on potentially can shift. Our attention may deepen, becoming more focused. Or it may turn toward something else.

Mindful attention is to be present to something or someone, whatever you are engaged with at the moment. We pay attention to what we choose to pay attention to, while allowing other stimuli to remain in the background.

Putting your attention on something can be an active choice. Meeting a friend in a busy restaurant, we may focus our attention on the conversation we are having and disregard extraneous noises in the background.

We do many things without mindful attention. In fact, we do most things automatically, without noticing or tracking how we did what we did.

As we brush our teeth, our attention might be on the music we are hearing, or we may be thinking about a task we have yet to do. While eating dinner, our attention might be on a device screen, a television program, or remembering something that upset us earlier in the day. Eating on automatic, we may not even notice, much less appreciate the taste of the meal as much as we could, were we to stop and put our attention on it.

Some research suggests that ninety-eight percent of what we do is automatic. Automaticity is useful, in that it is impossible to pay simultaneous attention to everything at once. Automaticity allows us to put our attention on novelty and respond to it, even as we are doing another activity more or less automatically.

However, when your mindful attention is on what you are doing in the moment, you are being present to the moment. This is extremely useful when you are examining your thought patterns and when you want to explore your emotional processes more deeply.

Intentions vs Goals

Let me differentiate what I will mean in this book by *having an intention* from *having a goal.*

- A *goal* is concerned with achieving a specific and tangible outcome. This can involve a behavior.
- An *intention* is concerned with how we want to *be* with whatever we put attention on—or as we move towards a goal.

Say my goal is to go to the market. An intention about doing this could include, "I want to be more present to my experience." This intention will affect my awareness. I might walk more slowly and take in more of my environment. Once in the store, my attention may be more focused, rather than losing myself looking at items that I am not going to buy.

As you set your intention, you bring awareness and direction to your experience in the moment.

Here's another example of how I set an intention. My goal was to take a walk. My intention was to be spontaneous. I started letting my feet lead the way.

I once explored San Francisco with the intention of spontaneity, and ended up discovering side-streets with incredible murals. I didn't have a specific goal other than taking a walk. But the outcome revealed itself as I walked.

So one may act with intention without aiming for an outcome, allowing outcomes to be revealed as one remains present to one's experience in the moment.

Getting Rid of Something

When asked about their intentions, many clients say they want to *get rid* of depression or anxiety. While understandable, this is actually a poorly-formed intention that seldom leads to insight or transformation.

In fact, it usually only makes things worse.

As an alternative to trying to get rid of it, we can first imagine what might be on the other side of depression and anxiety. Let's say the other side is that I am living my life more fully, where I am doing the things I want to do and meeting the people I want to meet (goal). Notice that goal involves my aiming to reach a tangible destination.

But in addition to my destination (my goal), there is the vital matter of how I get there—that moment-to-moment process of what happens internally within me as I take each step. What is the journey itself like?

That can be influenced by my intentions.

Here's what might happen. As I imagine that goal, I might start feeling discouraged because it seems impossible to reach it right now. So what might my intention be for the journey?

Let's say that I want to experience a state of calmness. I might identify that, to me on a deeper level, calmness is rooted in self-acceptance.

So I might say, "I want to be able to feel calm. I want to be able to accept myself." Okay! As soon as I have this intention, I can be more curious about my journey. I can say, "Along the way, I want to accept myself or I want to explore and work with whatever prevents me from accepting myself."

This intention fosters a willingness to be with my experience and sense into it. Now my attention has a clear focus. Ideally, I want to live my life more fully (goal), and along the way I am curious about what makes it hard for me to achieve the state of calmness and self-acceptance (intention). I am willing to be with my experience as I inquire about these matters.

If I had stayed solely with the goal of wanting to live my life fully, having great work, and meeting exciting new people—with no intention of inquiry—my attention might automatically lead to a negative thought and take me down a counter-productive path. I might start feeling hopeless. As I have not really inquired about the deeper levels of what is driving the hopelessness it will be more likely to be lost and not to find a way back.

With no intention about the journey itself I might miss the opportunity to inquire into deeper layers of myself. But if I stay with my intention to engage in a process of inquiry about this, even if I feel discouraged or hopeless, I can hold my experience and thereby my attention will continue to support me to be on my journey consciously.

Joining Intention with Inquiry

When we consciously direct our attention with intention, we can engage in a rich process of inquiry.

As we inquire, we will receive information from whatever we put our attention on—from outside or inside of us.

If we stay with whatever arises, the state we are in will start revealing itself more deeply…

And eventually there will be a shift.

If we are engaging in inquiry with a clear intention, the goal we thought was so distant might flicker nearby during the process. We may even notice that as we are in the process of inquiry, we start having access to what we thought was so far away.

It is paradoxical that when we embrace and get interested in our inner states that we initially wanted to get rid of, we open the doors of transformation.

So, one powerful way to transform inner states is to bring our attention to them with the intention of engaging in inquiry. Inquiry can be done in many ways: intellectually, artistically, emotionally.

Inquiry also includes noticing body sensations that arise within us as we experience an inner state. In noticing, we accept these sensations as they are and we get interested in describing and tracking how they may change over time.

As sensations are like the molecules of emotions, the act of putting attention on them and engaging in this form of somatic inquiry can open a door that will enable the sensations—and corresponding inner energetic state—to start to shift.

Tracking the subtle changes in body sensations can increase the potential that they will flow and begin to transform or shift the state we experience.

Sensing your inner "yes" or "no"...

To hear me guide you through this exercise, use this link:

hazalselcuk.com/tunnel-exercises

Or do the exercise as you read the following. Let's start with a simple experiment about noticing your body sensations...

- *Please make a fist and tighten it. Just hold it very tight…*
- *As you hold it tight, how does your hand feel?*
- *Does it feel tight or relaxed… warm or cold… heavy or light… hard or soft…*
- *Slowly open the fist and place your palm on your leg, lap or knee… or anywhere that feels comfortable.*
- *Let your hand just rest there…*
- *How does your hand feel now?*
- *Tight, relaxed, warm, cold, heavy, light, hard, soft…*

Now let's explore the signals your body gives you when it is saying "yes" vs "no" to something…

Imagine you are shopping for a used car. You go to car lot number one. You don't see anything you like. Then a salesman comes up to you. He starts saying how great the car you are standing next to is.

Meanwhile you are thinking, "What junk. Look at all that rust… bent up fenders… this is totally ridiculous… obviously it has been in a car wreck."

The salesman continues telling you how great this car is. Then he finally asks, "I can make you a real good deal on this one. Let's talk numbers and see if you can drive this home today... Okay?"

He stands there waiting for an answer...

- *Notice what your body is saying.*
- *What sensations do you feel?*
- *Where do you feel them?*
- *Are the sensations in your body saying "yes" or a "no"?*

Next, you walk across the street to car lot number two. You look around and there it is, the car of your dreams! You go over to it. Then a salesman comes up to you. He starts saying how great the car is.

Meanwhile you are thinking, "Wow... This car is what I was dreaming of.... It's absolutely immaculate! Not a scratch on it. Brand new tires. And it's even in my favorite color..."

The salesman continues telling you how great this car is. Then he finally asks, "I can make you a real good deal on this one. Let's talk numbers and see if you can drive this home today...Okay?"

He stands there waiting for an answer...

- *Notice what your body is saying.*
- *What sensations do you feel?*
- *Where do you feel them?*

- *Are the sensations in your body saying "yes" or a "no"?*
- *Reflect on the sensations you felt with these two salesmen. How did they feel different?*
- *Did one feel tight vs the other feeling relaxed somewhere in your body?*
- *Was one heavy vs the other feeling light?*
- *Was one warm and the other cool?*
- *Was one heavy vs the other feeling light?*
- *Was there more energy moving in one?*
- *Did your body seem to want to move toward vs wanting to get away?*
- *What other differences did you notice?*
- *Do you usually notice how your body says "yes" vs "no"?*

Just Because You Think It Doesn't Make It True

A powerful arena of inquiry involves noticing and questioning our thoughts and feelings. Most of us may take our thoughts and feelings for granted as being accurate and true. But just because you think it doesn't make it true.

A great deal of what we think and feel—as well as what pulls our attention—is generated automatically by unconscious processes within us. And these are often biased toward the negative. If you simply accept such thoughts as true, you will only get misled into feeling worse.

But if you operate from a conscious intention, you can take an active role in directing your attention. You can question and bring curiosity to your own thoughts and feelings. This is the very essence of the process of inquiry.

Inquiry can be done verbally. It can also be done creatively. As an example, let's say my attention is pulled to the thought, "I am a bad person." I may automatically believe that I actually am a bad person just because I had that thought. That negative thought, left unquestioned, will then evoke a negative feeling in me. Perhaps I will feel very sad.

Now, I have the thought, "I am bad," and a feeling of sadness or maybe anger. This will move me towards an action. If I don't know how to be with my emotions, maybe I will want to hide in bed or I will yell in face of a slightest trigger.

These actions may further feed the thought, "I am a bad person." Hence, I will continue feeling sadder—maybe even ashamed. And then I probably will want to hide or yell more. Do you see how I can get caught in an automatic loop?

It all started when I reacted to a negative thought without any inquiry. This gave the thought enormous power over me.

But let's now say that I have a clear intention to *explore* what drives the thought that "I am a bad person." My deliberate intention of inquiry will enable me to actively direct my attention in a more productive direction.

The process of inquiry at first could be very simple. It could go something like this. I simply observe the thought, "I am a bad person." Then I might say to myself, "I notice that I have the thought that I am a bad person. When I have that thought, I feel very sad. I wonder what is going on?"

This inquiry can generate a different path of action. Maybe I will do research and find a book on negative thinking patterns or on trauma. Maybe I'll talk to a friend or a therapist. I may write about it, I may draw. I may engage in intentional movement.

Rather than automatically believing the thought "I am a bad person," I will now be able to direct my attention on it and engage in a process of inquiry. My intention of doing this helps me go deeper into whatever I aim to become more aware of, and not just accept a negative thought as being true.

As mentioned above, a process of inquiry may consist of questions, or a creative process such as drawing, writing, sounding, or movement to explore feelings and thoughts. It can involve metaphors, images, and symbols.

As I become more aware, and with intention, I can choose to delve more deeply into my inquiry and explore the emotional dynamics that may be driving my thought pattern. I can choose to be with my sadness. Intention is like a rope that I can hold onto while I dive into the depths of my own psyche to inquire about my experiences and then climb back up.

Holding onto this rope of intention, I will not get lost. I will not drown in a thought or overwhelming emotion. My intention helps me organize and contain my experience so that I can gain more clarity and insight into my truth.

It is possible to develop the skills to move and redirect your attention. Out of this, your inner-knowing will be deepened and you can experience more choice and possibility.

The following sections offer ways to direct your attention that can transform your experience of daily life and give you a sense of agency over what otherwise may be automatic processes that drive overwhelming symptoms.

Directing Attention

At any time, we can become aware of where our attention is focused. Right now as I write "I am aware that my attention is on a sound of a dog barking." Our attention could be on something that we see. It could be on a thought, a feeling, or a body sensation.

Such things are the *content* of our awareness. Whenever we notice that our attention has become fixed on some particular content, we could claim our power to move our attention to something else. That is, we could actively choose where to place our focus.

In this way we can strengthen our ability to be aware of the direction of our attention—and increase our ability to shift where we put it—as opposed to getting lost in content that is having a negative impact on us.

Experiencing anxiety or depression can often be like getting lost or overcome by difficult weather. Metaphorically, lightning storms of anxiety or dark clouds of depression may seem like they are taking us over entirely. But if we direct our attention consciously, a shift can occur and our awareness can broaden. We can then more easily stay grounded in ourselves despite the lightning or dark clouds.

Instead of getting lost in the clouds, we can sense the sky that the clouds pass through. In that way, we broaden our sense of self to be more like the sky itself—larger than any particular distressing weather patterns that move through us.

We can even choose to inquire more deeply about any particular cloud that comes along. We could explore the feeling and embodiment of it, write about it, sound it, talk about it, or feel into it. And we are able to do this from a broader perspective of being the sky that holds the cloud. Thus, we don't get lost in the cloud. In this way, our inquiry might also lead to a movement of the cloud, perhaps even revealing a ray of sunshine in the process.

When we develop our capacity to direct our attention, we cultivate a power of choice. Instead of just automatically getting caught up in our thoughts or feelings, it is empowering to simply observe our thoughts or feelings and stay grounded in our present-moment awareness.

Differentiating from Thoughts and Feelings

As we get better at developing our power to direct our attention, we will strengthen our ability to differentiate ourselves from those thoughts and feelings that are the content of our awareness.

Again, we can self-identify as the sky instead of the patterns of weather that move through the sky. We can develop the capacity to be with our experiences in a way that we don't have to get swept away by them every time the weather changes.

This capacity is about containing and expressing feelings, not judging but questioning our thoughts, especially the negative ones that typically accompany depression and anxiety.

Differentiating ourselves from the thoughts and feelings that move through us increases our ability to contain or express these thoughts and feelings.

Knowing we are the sky through which thoughts and feelings rise and set, we will become more facile in handling them, getting their deeper messages, while staying grounded in the present. This enables us to exercise more resourceful options rather than simply getting swept away by thoughts and feelings to the point that we are completely at their mercy.

Pendulating Attention

Think of a pendulum as something that swings back and forth between two extremes. A child on a swing set is an example—swinging back and forth.

Our nervous system pendulates naturally. Our natural need is to be able to go into a state of excitement and high energy and then to come back to a state of rest and relaxation. It is like day and night. We need action. Then we need rest.

Society doesn't put high value on resting, so our nervous systems tend to get continuously stimulated. Many of us can get stuck in the mode of hyperarousal and excitement. Missing the natural balance that includes rest, this can eventually keep our systems in a loop of increasing anxiety. On the other hand, if we are depressed, our nervous system can get stuck in the low energy mode of hypoarousal and shut down.

When we learn to direct our attention to move from one thing to another, we can increase our ability to track inner states and subtle shifts inside of us that may be pointing us towards restoring balance.

By mindfully directing our attention, we can learn to track and embody a natural process of pendulation—for instance, we move from intense to more calming content, or from a collapsed state to a more energized state.

As we engage and play with moving our attention, we can also strengthen our ability to shift between depressive content to more resourceful content—or between anxious content to more relaxing content.

For example, you could potentially shift your attention from a depressed thought looping in your mind and choose to place your attention on a flower.

Similarly, you could shift your attention from anxious thoughts streaming through your mind and put your attention on feeling the earth beneath your feet—or sensing the warmth of the sun on your face. This can begin to give you a sense of control. Then when you chose you can also explore the deeper emotional layers.

Symptoms don't have to guide and control the content of your awareness. You can claim your ability to direct your own attention. And engaging in this active attentional shift may also create a shift of your inner state and give you the mental space to inquire more deeply into yourself.

Shifting your focus...

To hear me guide you through this exercise, use this link:

hazalselcuk.com/tunnel-exercises

Or do the exercise as you read the following page. Please do this exercise sitting down...

- *Think of a negative thought, a worry, a judgement, something upsetting... This could be a thought about you, about a situation or about someone else.*
- *What do you sense physically in your body when you think of that thought?*
- *Describe any body sensations you notice: tightness, lightness, closing, opening, expansion, heaviness, warmth, coolness, buzzing, tingling...*

- *Where do you notice these sensations? In what part or what parts of your body?*
- *Now shift your focus to feeling where your pelvis makes contact with the chair or whatever you are sitting on.*
- *Feel your sitting bones.*
- *Feel how the chair or what you are sitting on is holding you, holding your weight.*
- *How does your pelvis feel? Heavy, light, solid, wide, tight, relaxed...*
- *Now return to the negative thought again.*
- *As you think of that thought just notice what happens in your body...*
- *What sensations seem to be shifting, changing, or coming back again?*
- *What part or parts of your body do you feel more now?*
- *Finally, return to feeling your seat again and just notice again how you are being held by the chair or whatever is holding you.*
- *Feel your weight being held.*
- *As you feel the contact with the chair what sensations do you notice now? Wide, open, tight, narrow, closed, heavy, light, solid...*

The Cycle of Thought, Feeling and Action

Let's reiterate the relationship between thoughts, feelings, and actions. An emotional state feeds thought. Thoughts feed emotions. That exchange may result in physical action, or lack thereof. Actions and feelings create memories. And memory projects what we expect to happen in the future.

In order to open up space for change, it is useful to deconstruct what is happening on a mental, emotional, behavioral and bodily level. This will enable you to understand what produces any given state, mental conclusion or physical action.

So, let's first inquire into how a depressed state may be operating on a mental and physical level.

Say that I am slouching, looking down, moving slowly, or not moving at all. Then, sooner or later, I find myself in an emotional state that corresponds to the physical shape and rhythm I am in. It would be very hard to sustain a sense of joy in the physical posture I just described, as it would be hard to slouch, look down, and move slowly if we were truly joyful.

Often an emotional state generates a physical posture, and each feeds the other. An emotional state will generate certain muscular and thought patterns, which again reinforce that state.

To break the cycle of negative states, we can put awareness on our thoughts—or on our body. That is, we can start examining our cognitive content and inquire into negative thought patterns that feed a negative state. Or we can track the state of our body by getting in touch with the physical sensations in our body. We call the latter *somatic listening.*

The exercises presented above in this chapter are examples of somatic listening.

Note, the word "soma" means *body* in Greek.

A somatic approach offers great power in working with anxiety or depression. By cultivating our body awareness, we open up space for energy to flow within our body. This will impact our thoughts as well as our inner states.

When engaging in somatic listening, we will foster an increased sense of flow. That may result in our bodily expression in the form of movement. Movement can shift our emotional states, thought patterns, and actions. In this way, we start an upward spiral from which we could engage in deeper inquiry.

Let's continue our example.

So, you wake up feeling an emotional symptom of depression, let's say you are not motivated to do anything (state). You tell yourself that you don't want to get up, you want to stay in bed (thought). Say, then, you decide to stay in bed (action).

If you next tell yourself, "I am such a bad and lazy person that I'm not worthy of anything," your thoughts will take your symptoms to a deeper level. Your thoughts will intensify your negative emotional state. And your physical body will reflect the intensified negative state you are in. You are caught in a downward spiral.

So let's explore what would happen if you were to choose to slightly alter how you relate to the depression. Here you might tell yourself, "I will treat this like a kind of flu and stay in bed and take care of myself." With this slight change of thinking and intention, let's say you then decide to intervene on a bodily level as a form of self-care.

You may still decide to stay in bed, but now part of you wants to take care of yourself. Maybe you choose to put your hand on your heart. Maybe you cry a little. Or you cover yourself in a way that feels like care and compassion.

What might that change in how you see things?

Maybe then you would decide to call a friend, feel like taking a shower, or want to listen to a piece of music. You may still feel the symptoms. However, you will now have a different relationship to them as well as to yourself.

What would that be like?

Another possibility is that you may wake up depressed, hearing the thoughts, "I want to stay in bed," and then you choose to engage in a different action. You opt to take a shower and get involved in some activity. You may decide to go out into the world. You may just go for a walk and look at some flowers along your journey. You may stop along the way at a place for a cup of coffee or tea.

As you move through your day, you could have the intention to track how your emotional states might be shifting. At some point, you might decide to spend some time inquiring within yourself, "What drives this depression in me? What are the deeper emotional layers?"

You might also refine your ability to notice how the state shifts slightly from moment to moment, depending on where you put your attention and how you relate to yourself.

As you decide to change your relationship to depression, your posture, rhythm, perspective might also shift as everything in us is connected. What would that be like for you?

Directing your attention...

It's best to do this exercise with eyes closed. Thus listening to the online audio will be very helpful for this exercise. Find it using this link:

hazalselcuk.com/tunnel-exercises

If you are not comfortable with your eyes being closed or if you cannot listen to the audio, then just do the exercise by reading through it below.

Doing it this way may not be quite as easy as simply listening to it being guided, but you will still be able to experience directing your attention.

- *Please sit or lie down.*
- *Think of a thought that bothers you. Just pick any one thought.*
- *As you think of that thought what body sensations do you notice?*
- *Do you feel any tightness, tension, tingling, heaviness, or any other sensation?*
- *Does it evoke a feeling?*
- *If you can, close your eyes.*
- *Bring your attention to your pelvis.*
- *Feel the contact your pelvis is making with the surface you are sitting or lying on.*
- *How does your pelvis feel—heavy, light, solid?*
- *Then move your attention to your feet.*
- *If they are making contact with a surface, feel that contact. Otherwise notice whatever they*

are making contact with—socks, air, blanket, whatever...

- *Now, push your feet against the floor or any other surface you can make contact with.*
- *If you are laying down you may have to bend your knees to feel the soles of your feet making contact with a surface or floor. Or you can push against a wall.*
- *Push and feel your legs. Then let go.*
- *Again, push and feel your legs. Then let go.*
- *Notice if there is any other movement your body wants to do right now. Just freely explore how your body might want to move for about a minute.*
- *Now, put one hand on your belly and one hand on your chest. Just put your attention on your breathing.*
- *Track each in-breath and out-breath.*
- *Notice the rising and falling of your chest as you inhale and exhale.*
- *Continue tracking your breath for a minute.*
- *Now, what sensations do you feel in your body? Where in your body do you feel this?*

- *Does it feel soft, light, warm, tense, alive, relaxed, comfortable, tingling, contracted, buzzing, heavy, cold, constricted?*
- *Find a specific sensation in your body that feels good to feel.*
- *Stay focused on that sensation and let it build up in strength if it wants to. If it dissipates then find another sensation that feels good and track it.*
- *If a pleasant sensation is strong enough, then recall that unpleasant thought you had at the start of this exercise.*
- *How do you relate to that thought from this place?*
- *Do you go right back to it?*
- *Are you experiencing some distance?*
- *Is there anything else you notice?*

Which Emotion Is Not Safe to Feel?

Emotions are "energy in motion" that arise out of our subjective responses to life's experiences. We feel happy when our team wins the game. We become frustrated when we can't find our keys. We grieve when we lose someone we love. We feel joy when a baby is born.

Emotions have range and they carry messages to us. They may also indicate something about our environment. Here are some examples of what various emotions may signal:

Joy = An important need is being fulfilled.
Sadness = Something valuable seems lost.
Fear = Something seems dangerous.
Anger = A boundary has been crossed.
Compassion = Want to engage and help.

When we allow ourselves to feel and receive the messages of emotional states, we increase depth and connection within ourselves. To the extent we are able to connect with a feeling within our self, we will be able to connect with others when they have that feeling.

Thus, if we can feel our pain, we can be with another person's pain. Our ability to have and show *empathy* directly comes from our ability to connect to a similar feeling within ourselves.

Also, our ability to authentically feel and express joy will increase to the extent we can feel our emotional pain.

Emotional pain or pleasure might feel dangerous to some of us. We may have learned in the past that it is not safe to feel. Hence unconscious strategies for avoiding or masking pain may get automatically and subconsciously engaged.

Depression and anxiety often inhibit or block our ability to feel and receive the messages that our deeper emotions are trying to convey to us. Typically, this has corresponding consequences that not only reduce our capacity for empathy but also decrease the ability to feel true joy.

Why Not Just Take a Pill?

Patterns of being depressed or anxious may have been triggered by a recent overwhelming experience. Or they may have developed from earlier adverse experiences, as far back as infancy or childhood. They may be the result of another physical illness or side effects from a medication.

In some cases of depression or anxiety, especially if resulting from chemical imbalances in the brain, medication can help bring someone back to a more chemically balanced state. But a pill alone is not your most powerful option if the symptoms are driven by deeper emotional states that have roots in overwhelming life experiences.

Research shows that the combination of medications with therapy is more beneficial than medications alone. Therapy gives you the safe space to develop your ability to hear what these powerful states have to say.

Medication sometimes helps us come back to a place where we can begin to inquire within ourselves. And therapy helps us to feel into, hear and understand the "cry of the soul".

Symptoms of depression and anxiety develop when we don't feel safe in our own skin. This often occurs if our ability to feel our emotions or to assert our needs got blocked in the past, and we continue to operate unconsciously the same way today.

We can begin to shift unconscious patterns by engaging in inquiry, in the many ways discussed in this book. Instead of believing that we will stay stuck forever, we can question our negative thoughts and process our feelings.

It is always handy to remember that just because you *think* it does not make it *true*.

Even in the most stuck of times, we can still do the one thing always possible—to move our attention.

We can even move our body.

A powerful way to open up your system again includes movement in its many forms—from physical movement of your limbs, to enabling the movement and flow of your feelings, to the ability to direct and move your attention.

As your system starts naturally moving energy again—reinvigorating positive states as well—you will gradually recover the ability to make space for whatever is the opposite of depression or anxiety.

FINAL REFLECTIONS

"The possibility of change is available in every second."

— ANONYMOUS

We have explored depression and anxiety from many points of view. Let's review ways we have looked at these symptoms, with an emphasis on how to better relate to them.

- We first viewed depression and anxiety from the perspective of life energy—emphasizing the impact of trauma on the nervous system. These states represent energy that runs either too high (hyperarousal) or too low (hypoarousal).

- We also looked at the animal defenses that get triggered when we feel under survival threat and how these relate to depression and anxiety. The lock-up corresponds to anxiety, while collapse corresponds to depression.

- We further saw how our minds make overly-simplistic, negative meanings out of our internal experiences. We then explored the nature of meaning-making and the complexity inherent in depression and anxiety.

- We also took an artistic perspective on depression and anxiety—reframing both as a cry from the soul that needs a listening ear. And in doing so, we explored how to start listening to our own internal states.

- Then we explored several artforms—music, theater, movement, drawing—as a canvas for creativity and healing.

- We looked at depression and anxiety as having the potential to offer access to valuable personal material for emotional, mental and spiritual growth.

- We then examined attention, intention, and inquiry as tools for exploring feelings and thoughts—and for being connected to ourselves. We saw the power of inquiry to challenge and overcome debilitating states and negative internal narratives.

- We looked at the triad of thought-emotion-action and saw how attention can be a valuable tool to bring curiosity to emotional, mental, physical and behavioral experiences.

- Finally, we did some exercises that offer new ways for you to connect to your internal experiences and develop the sense of choice and agency in doing so.

What is the Light in the Tunnel?

Reflecting on the title of this book, the "light in the tunnel" is about bringing curiosity to inner aspects of ourselves. By cultivating our capacity to be with our inner experience, we can reconnect to a deeper sense of internal safety.

As infants, we expressed ourselves through our feelings.

For many of us, somewhere along the way—probably early on— we learned that this was not very safe to do.

That was true *then.*

But it need not remain so *today.*

You can gradually grow your capacity to feel, express, and contain your feelings and difficult internal states.

You can learn to understand their intended messages and what they are attempting to convey to you.

We do not have to remain in darkness.

By embracing our full human experience, we bring light into the tunnel. This book is meant to point you in that direction.

Valuable Questions to Take with You

Here are some useful questions to keep in mind when you get drawn into or overwhelmed by anxiety or depression.

Take some time to sit with these questions below:

- What do I want for myself?
- What is safe about being depressed?
- What is safe about being anxious?
- Can I imagine relating to depression and anxiety in a different way?
- When I allow myself to imagine this, what do I see, think, and feel?
- How comfortable am I around allowing myself to ask for support if I need it?
- Would it be useful to remember that my mind makes up negative stories? (Come up with a scenario and imagine remembering this.)

- How do I want to relate to the negative stories my mind makes up about me?
- Is it okay to cultivate a sense of safety inside and outside?
- Is it safe to say “no”?
- Is it safe to say “yes”?
- How do I feel about deciding to make my body move even if I don’t want to move?
- Is it okay to keep in mind that movement alters brain chemistry in positive ways?
- How do I feel about directing my mind away from negativity when I am overwhelmed?
- When do I think about play, like children do, without any concern about the outcome and yet being totally invested in it, what do I experience?

The 21-Day Program

Guided Audio Exercises for Anxiety and Depression

Clients often ask me for advice about what to do to overcome the symptoms of anxiety or depression. They ask if I would provide a few exercises they could practice so they can better manage the overwhelm. This is a valuable request and shows they are invested in experiencing shifts within themselves.

As a result of these requests, I included several brief exercises in this book. Some include links to online audio recordings that gave step-by-step guidance through that exercise.

Beyond the simple exercises you got in this book, I have created a *21-Day Program for Anxiety and Depression.*

In this online program I guide you through in-depth exercises that are designed to help you shift your internal state. The exercises also guide you in learning how to better manage and transform symptoms of depression or anxiety.

The program aims to help you enliven and bring balance to your inner sense of self. Each exercise is presented as an audio recording in which I will guide you to engage with your personal material in various ways. Each exercise is designed to provide you with specific experiences to proactively be with your internal states in new ways that are safe, fun and even creative.

The exercises build on each other. The program is largely experiential. Reading the book *A Light in the Tunnel* has given you all the theoretical background information you need for this program. Rather than discussing theories or ideas, this program was designed to give you new experiences that will increase your inner skills and sense of safety.

The program will support you to explore new ways for sensing and noticing feelings and reflecting on yourself. It was constructed to give you a sense of inner stability and help you towards working on deeper emotional material.

You can use this program prior to starting therapy, or it can go hand-in-hand with therapy. Or you may decide that the program gives you all of what you need for the moment.

Here is a link to more information online about the *21-Day Program for Anxiety and Depression:*

hazalselcuk.com/21-day-program

Bibliography

Atıcı, E. & Erer, S. (2010) *Selçuklu ve Osmanlılarda Müzikle Tedavi Yapılan Hastaneler*, Journal of Uludağ University Medical Faculty, Volume 36, Issue 1, 29-32

Caldwell, C. (2018) *Bodyfullness*, Shambala Publications, CO 80301

Campbell, S. & Grey, J. (2015) *Five-Minute Relationship Repair*, New World Library, Novato, CA 94949

Chödron, P. (2000) *When Things Fall Apart*, Shambala Publications, CO 80301

Emunah, R. (1994) *Acting for Real, Drama Therapy Process Technique and Performance*, Routledge Taylor and Frances Group, NY 10016

Feldenkreis, M. (2010) *Embodied Wisdom, The Collected Papers of Mosche Feldenkreis*, ed. by Beringer, E., Somatic Resources, CA 92103

Gersie, A., ed. (2007) *Dramatic Approaches to Brief Therapy*, Jessica Kingsley Publishers, PA 19106

Gibson, D. (2013) *The Complete Guide to Soundhealing*, Globe Sound and Consciousness Institute, CA

Halprin, D. (2003) *The Expressive Body in Life, Art and Therapy*, Jessica Kingsley Publishers, London

Heller, L. & La Pierre, H. (2012) *Healing Developmental Trauma*, North Atlantic Books, CA 94712

Kelemann, S. (1981) *Your Body Speaks its Mind*, Center Press, CA 94709

King, Juliet L., ed. (2016) *Art Therapy, Trauma and Neuroscience*, Routledge, NY 10017

Landy, R. (1994) *Drama Therapy, Concepts, Theories and Practices*, Charles C Thomas, IL 62794

Levine, P. (1997) *Waking the Tiger*, North Atlantic Books, CA 94712

Levine, P. (2010) *In an Unspoken Voice*, North Atlantic Books, CA 94712

Mahler, M., Pine, F. & Bergman, A. (1975) *The Psychological Birth of the Human Infant*, Basic Books, NY 10016

Malchiodi, C., ed. (2005) *Expressive Therapies*, The Guilford Press, NY 10012

Masterson, J. (2015) *Personality Disorders Through the Lens of Attachment Theory Neurobiologic Development of the Self*, Zeig, Tucker, Theisen, AZ 85016

Mayer, M. (2007) *Body Mind Healing Psychotherapy*, Body Mind Healing Publications, Orinda CA

Ogden, P. & Fisher J. (2015) *Sensorimotor Psychotherapy*, W. W. Norton & Company, NY 10110

Oğuzcan, Ü. (2008) *Aşka Dair Nesirler*, Everest Yayınları-Şiir Dizisi

Pallaro, P., ed. (1999) *Authentic Movement Essays by Starks Mary Whitehouse, Janet Adler & Joan Chodorow*, Jessica Kingsley Publishers, London

Schore, A. (2003) *Affect Dysregulation and Disorders of the Self*, W.W. Norton & Company, NY 10110

Schwartz, R. (1995) *Internal Family Systems Therapy*, The Guilford Press, NY 10001

Siegel, D. (2011) *Mindsight, The New Science of Personal Transformation,* Bantam Books by Random House, NY

Van der Kolk, B. (2014) *The Body Keeps the Score,* Penguin Books, NY 10014

Wallin, D. (2007) *Attachment in Psychotherapy,* The Guilford Press, NY 10001

About the Author

Hazal Selçuk, MA, MFA, LMFT, REAT, RSME/T, RDT, NARM Therapist, works with individuals and couples. She got her MA in Counseling Psychology at the California Institute of Integral Studies.

Hazal is a Registered Expressive Arts Therapist (REAT), a Registered Somatic Movement Educator and Therapist (RSME/T), and a Registered Drama Therapist (RDT). She is a Licensed Marriage and Family Therapist in the State of California (LMFT).

Hazal's clinical background includes working at Langley Porter Psychiatric Institute, the Center for Empowering Refugees, the Jewish Free Clinic, San Quentin Prison, the Lomi Psychotherapy Clinic, the Mind Therapy Clinic, Healing Couples Retreats, and the Mindful Heart Center.

Hazal was born in Paris to a family of artists.

After completing Austrian high school she then attended Center for Contemporary Music in Istanbul and studied musical theater at the State Conservatory of Vienna.

She earned a BFA from the Boston Conservatory, where she majored in musical theater and minored in movement and dance.

Hazal received an MFA from York University in Toronto. At York's theater department she specialized in performing movement theater, playmaking, and teaching movement for actors.

For years Hazal was a singer and solo performer. She also taught university classes on the relationship between artmaking and healing.

In addition to her practice in psychotherapy she currently creates and performs new compositions as well as singing and arranging musical works of her father and grandfather.

Having lived in five different countries and on three continents, she is adept at working with cross-cultural dynamics and issues within individuals and couples.

You can read articles, see Hazal's audiobooks, and learn more about the therapeutic and coaching services she provides by visiting her website:

hazalselcuk.com